INSTANT
GARDENING

ADAM & JAMES CAPLIN

Chatto & Windus
LONDON

Published in 1990 by

Chatto & Windus Limited
20 Vauxhall Bridge Road
London SW1V 2SA

A CIP catalogue record for this book is available
from the British Library.

ISBN 0 7011 3485 2

Illustrations by Kevin Dean

Typesetting by Rowland Phototypesetting Limited
Bury St Edmunds, Suffolk
Colour origination by Scan Trans – Singapore
Printed in Great Britain by
Butler & Tanner Limited, Frome, Somerset

INSTANT
GARDENING

To Mum and Dad

Acknowledgements

The authors would like to thank Julia Hobsbaum for all her early encouragement; Caradoc King, Richard Bird, Andrew Bailey for their expert help; Kevin Dean for his patience and wonderful illustrations; Richard Jackson, John Ravenscroft and the team at Chatto & Windus who made it all such fun. We are also grateful to everyone at the Garden Centres at Alexandra Palace and Hounslow Heath for their support.

Contents

Introduction

Pleasure, excitement and fun are important parts of Instant Gardening. For too long, gardening has been made to seem a serious and difficult business, weighed down by long Latin names and detailed horticultural knowledge. This makes most people feel as if they don't know enough to garden properly. But you don't need to be such an expert to enjoy gardening. In this book we have tried to make the whole thing more fun.

Traditional gardening is based on ideas that are rarely acknowledged, let alone questioned – for example, that people spend many years living in one house and working on one garden. So the ideal for the traditional gardener is a 'mature' garden: a patch of paradise representing decades of continuous work in which trees, shrubs, bulbs and bedding plants have finally achieved a balance with each other.

But most of us now expect to move house several times. Planting a young apple tree and waiting years for it to fruit seems pointless: it will only benefit the next people to live there.

Traditional gardening also puts plants first. That is why the emphasis is on maintaining the perfect lawn, on growing the flawless rose, on cultivating superb fruit. Instant Gardening makes a new assumption: that the garden should be primarily for people.

So instead of describing how to make a perfect lawn, we outline how different sorts of lawn satisfy different needs and describe how to make them. After all, if you want a garden that is attractive to wildlife, your ideal lawn will be very different to that of a croquet fanatic.

So this book is not filled with glorious photographs of stunning plants and wonderful gardens. Pictures like that assume that what you want is the idealised garden and that you have unlimited time, skill and money. Instead, the illustrations in this book aim to give an idea of what is possible. How you put them into practice is part of the pleasure and excitement of Instant Gardening.

At the very least, we trust that after reading this book, you'll never garden the same way again.

CHAPTER ONE

What is Your Garden For?

Merely asking the question seems bizarre. Surely you want your garden to be a place where you can sunbathe and relax, do recreational gardening, grow fresh fruit and vegetables, allow the children to run riot and the dog to exercise, watch wildlife...

Unfortunately in an average-sized garden with a normal bank balance and only 24 hours in a day, you can only do a limited number of things.

So how do you answer the question?

Imagine you have a small garden. Your children love to play in it – especially close to a treasured, rare specimen. After years of careful nurturing, just as it is about to flower, a wildly-kicked football scythes off the only budded branch. Although you pamper the lawn, it doesn't look that good because they've worn a bare patch between the goalposts. You have a couple of cherry trees but, in spite of all the precautions you take, most of the fruit is taken by the birds.

You could approach these problems in a traditional way. You lose your temper with the children, re-seed the lawn for the umpteenth time and put a hefty frame around the fruit trees.

The only trouble is, this won't work. The garden has become a focus for domestic friction and no longer a place to be enjoyed; the delicate young grass shoots last no longer than their predecessors; and nothing you do seems to discourage the birds.

It is not surprising that you're having problems. You want a lot from this garden and there are some obvious clashes (children and delicate plants is one; wildlife and fruit another).

The Instant Gardening solution is to start by deciding what you want your garden for. Maybe it should be for growing fruit; or perhaps it should be somewhere outdoors and safe for the kids to play; or for attracting wildlife.

Now you need to put what you want into order of priority. Perhaps you decide the most important is for the garden to be a place where the children can play; next comes attracting wildlife, then growing fruit.

Your children are punishing the lawn – so let it grow longer. This will make it more hardwearing and, if you include some wildflowers, it will be welcoming for birds and insects.

Planting delicate specimens near where the children play is asking for trouble. Either arrange protection for the plants, or move them to a less vulnerable position.

Since attracting wildlife is a priority, stop fighting the birds and enjoy them.

So, by putting your needs in order of priority, a plan begins to emerge.

This is the crucial first step in making an Instant Garden.

Case study one: before

These case studies are based on real gardens that we have Instant Gardened.

A busy young couple with a 3-year-old son have recently moved into a newly-built house, part of a large development.

All the gardens are bare except for a single tree planted in each. In this case it is a spring-flowering cherry, *Prunus* 'Kanzan'.

The land falls away from the house. There is a fence at the end of the garden, beyond which is a large park filled with trees.

The garden is sunniest near the house and shady at the end.

The couple have bought a sturdy swing for their son. It now dominates the garden.

Their sitting room is on the first floor and has a balcony.

Original plan

- Move earth from the end of the garden to near the house to make two flat terraces.

- Build a brick retaining wall to hold the banked-up earth in place.

- Turf the level nearest the house.

- Pave the end of the garden to make a patio.

- Build a permanent barbeque at the end of the garden.

The INSTANT GARDENING analysis

This helped them decide that their priorities were:

- a safe place for their son to play.

- a place for sunbathing.

- a garden that looked good from the house.

- fresh herbs and soft fruit.

- a barbeque area.

It was obvious that their original plans were not going to produce the garden they wanted.

Levelling the slope

The lawn wouldn't be a safe place for their son to play because of the drop onto the patio.

The patio

Because the patio was to be in the shadier part of the garden, they would tend to sit on the lawn in the summer which would suffer.

Herbs

There is little room in this scheme for flower beds – let alone for herbs and fruit.

The barbeque area

Putting it at the end of the garden isn't very practical. Not only is it far from the kitchen, it's also in the shade.

The surroundings

Seen from the house, the garden would contrast strongly with the park.

Case study one: after

Using the principles of Instant Gardening, the couple thought about what they wanted their garden for and were then able to plan it with that in mind.

A safe place for their child to play

Slopes are safe and interesting for children so in this case it was an advantage rather than a problem. Keeping the slope rather than levelling it saved both time and money.

The swing was an eyesore and too big to screen. So one of the legs was put into a bed, where it could be used as a frame on which to grow a climber.

A place for sunbathing

The patio was put next to the house. This was both sunnier and more convenient.

This also meant they could keep an eye on their son from inside the house while he played on it.

A garden that looks good all year round

The cherry tree was fairly large which gave a sense of instant maturity to the garden. To increase its interest throughout the year, a summer-flowering climber was grown up it. They used a *Clematis 'jackmanii'* (dark blue flowers throughout the summer).

The view from the house

The most important view was from the sitting room on the first floor. From here the first thing in the garden you noticed was the back fence.

This was covered with a climbing plant which made it look as though the park was an extension of the garden. Since they would look at this throughout the year, the ideal choice was a quick-growing evergreen climber like *Akebia quinata* (a twining evergreen with soft green leaves).

6

Fresh herbs and soft fruit

The most convenient place for herbs is near the house. Since this is sunny, it is perfect for them. Where possible, the couple used ornamental herbs in the borders.

But soft fruit presents more of a problem. You have to devote quite a bit of time and space to fruit plants to get good crops. This couple were short of spare time. Also, many soft fruit plants have thorns, which aren't ideal when there is a very young child around. However, there are a couple of varieties of blackberry ('Oregon Thornless' and 'Merton Thornless') that have no thorns. They also have attractive foliage so are well suited to this garden.

In years to come, when their child has grown up and become less demanding and less vulnerable, the couple will be able to grow a greater variety of fruit.

The barbeque area

As this is a fairly small garden, it would not be sensible to build a permanent barbeque. Better to buy a portable one.

CONCLUSION

Even at this early stage, the couple felt much happier and more confident with the way their garden was developing. The Instant Gardening route also saved them time and money because they didn't have to move earth or build a retaining wall.

Case study two: before

A recently retired couple, with time to spare but limited money, realised that they weren't happy with their present garden.

It is quite large, with a big lawn, mature trees in the borders and a rockery in the shade. In one corner there's a garden shed.

They felt that the borders needed too much work and that weeds seemed to do better than the plants. When they put in new plants, they just disappeared into the background. Also, the lawn suffered where it was shaded by the trees.

Original plan

- To cut down on weeding, they had planted some ground cover: the Rose of Sharon *Hypericum calycinum* (a very rampant evergreen with lots of yellow flowers) and *Pachysandra terminalis* (an evergreen which is particularly suitable for shady areas).

- To hide their neighbours' houses, they were thinking about putting trellis along the top of the fence.

- They were also considering putting a panel of trellis in front of the shed. They planned to cover it with a fast growing climber like Russian vine *Polygonum baldschuanicum* (an extremely fast-growing, deciduous climber with foamy white flowers in mid to late summer).

- They put several fruit trees near the back of the garden.

The INSTANT GARDENING analysis
This helped them decide that their priorities were:

- a garden that was easy to maintain, but one in which there was still something to do.

- to be able to sit in the house and look out at an attractive view.

- to hide the neighbours' houses from view.

- to be able to eat home-grown fruit.

It was clear that their original plans didn't go far enough.

Groundcover
The hypericum was doing well but, unfortunately, weeds had already overwhelmed and killed the pachysandra. So there was still space in the beds for weeds to come up – and plenty of weeding to do.

Trellis
Putting trellis on the fence would be expensive and, until covered in plants, would draw the eye and so emphasise the view of the neighbours' houses. A panel of trelliis in front of the shed would do the same.

The fruit trees
These had been planted in a fairly shady area. As a result, they didn't produce a good crop.

9

Case study two: after

Using the principles of Instant Gardening, the couple made their plans by referring to their priorities.

To reduce the regular work in their garden

A large lawn takes regular work. Since this one is suffering under the mature trees, they replaced it in the shadiest parts with shrubs and ground cover that like shade. These will thrive and be easy to maintain.

As for the rest of the lawn, they put bulbs in the areas furthest from the house and let the grass grow longer there. This further reduces the burden of lawn maintenance without making the garden look too unruly.

To improve the view from the house

This is particularly important in winter because, during the colder months, the couple spend most of their time indoors. So they moved the winter flowering-plants to positions visible from the living room. This way they give maximum pleasure at the bleakest times of year.

To hide the shed, they planted a large evergreen in front of it, in this case the fire thorn *Pyracantha* 'Mohave' (an evergreen wall shrub particularly good in shade, with orange-red berries through autumn). They planted a contrasting specimen to one side of this to draw the eye *away* from the shed, *Weigela florida* 'Variegata' (a lovely shrub with green and white variegated leaves and pink flowers in June).

10

How to hide the neighbours' houses

The best and most cost effective way would be to plant more trees. Since the couple want a low-maintenance garden, these have to be fairly large specimens of varieties which will not need heavy pruning in the future – when the couple will be even less keen on heavy work.

Fruit

They moved the existing fruit trees to sunnier positions. In their place, they planted a morello cherry which doesn't mind shade.

A large, unruly, pear tree needed radical pruning. A professional tree surgeon was hired to reshape it to allow light and air into the centre. Pruning in the future will not be a big job and could probably be done by the couple.

The borders

To solve the problem of plants disappearing into the borders, instead of dotting them around, they clumped them together. This gives instant maturity, much greater impact and, when groundcover is needed, helps the groundcover plants get established and beat the weeds.

This means that when shopping for plants, they had to buy at least three of a small number of varieties rather than buying just one of a larger number of varieties.

Good plants for this couple were ones which looked after themselves and spread well – lady's mantle *Alchemilla mollis* (a herbaceous spreading plant with light green foliage and foamy, light green flowers in late spring); herbaceous geraniums (these come in a variety of delicate colours, are very hardy and good spreaders) and, for colour in late summer, in the shadier positions, astilbes (feathery foliage with plumes of white, pink or red flowers).

Case study two – conclusion

By following the Instant Gardening route, this couple achieved the garden they wanted – one which didn't require regular work, but in which there was always something light and interesting for them to do. And, once again, they saved time and money: by not having to buy and fix trellis and by avoiding frequent buying of plants which didn't make an impact.

Their garden began to look more informal and they realised they could make an Instant woodland glade (trees around a soft, meadowy lawn). To do this they would simply plant more bulbs in the lawn (clumps of crocus and daffodils) and put informal plants in the borders (hardy fuchsias, mock orange, campanulas).

At some time in the future, they may well lose the rockery so that the garden is completely integrated. The informality of their new garden also helps reduce the amount of regular work that is needed.

All it took was some thought, a few days' work and one visit from a professional (the tree surgeon).

SUMMARY

If you are not one of the green-fingered few, or don't have much time to lavish on your garden, it can easily become a focus for guilt. You'll feel you're neglecting it, and, as the burden of guilt increases, you'll probably find reasons for not gardening.

But with the Instant Gardening approach, which puts people first, it's much easier to enjoy your garden. With less guilt, and with a garden that suits the way you live, you'll probably use it more. And then, who knows, you might even end up wanting to do more gardening.

CHAPTER TWO

What Have You Got?

We all notice the bad things in our gardens: a weak view here; a sick tree there; a bad patch of lawn. But for some reason, most of us aren't able to appreciate what is good about them.

Using the hidden strengths of a garden is a very Instant Gardening way of improving what you've got.

Your garden and its surroundings

First ask yourself how your garden fits in with what's around it.

Views from the garden

Check for good views (trees in a neighbour's garden, a distant church spire). Where in the garden do you see them from? After all, a good view is useless if it is only really visible from the middle of the compost heap.

Could you reveal a good view if you moved something that is in the way?

Note the bad views, and where you see them from.

View from the house

The view from the house is vital, since most of us spend a lot of time indoors looking out.

Access

Access is important for many of the bigger jobs in the garden. If you can't get directly to the garden from the road without going through the house, can you get materials over an extension, over the back wall, even over a neighbour's wall?

Where access is only through the house, be prepared to put some effort into clearing the way and protecting the decor.

If you have just moved in, or plan to redecorate both house and garden, move the heavy materials into the garden before you redecorate the room that gives on to it.

Cats and squirrels

These are territorial and, if your garden is on their patch, they will exercise their rights over it. Cat excrement will damage plants to the point of killing them. Squirrels eat most fruit and some bulbs (tulips are a particular favourite).

You can discourage them by growing plants they don't like. Groundcover roses deter both squirrels and cats.

Neighbours

Who overlooks you, whom do you overlook? How do you feel about this? Many people find it more irritating to watch *them* barbequeing, than to be watched by them. This is most important in the sitting-out area.

Wind

You can make use of breezes, because there are plants that move very nicely in the wind. But strong wind can damage plants.

Light

Which areas are sunny and when do they get the sun? Most people like to sit out in the sun, so you will have to plan around it.

Are any areas particularly shady? Too many people treat shade as a problem and struggle with it. A shady area represents a great opportunity: there are lots of beautiful shade-loving plants, many of which can't be grown satisfactorily in sunny places (dwarf cyclamens, camellias, hostas and many more).

If you don't want the shade, are there trees or shrubs blocking the light that could be cut back?

Noise

Is there a major source of unpleasant noise nearby (a busy road or an airport)? Careful planting of suitable trees (for instance, *Populus tremula*) can reduce its effect.

The structure of your garden

What is your garden like as a whole?

Size and shape

You can't change the boundaries of your garden but you can change the way it *seems*. Different layouts create different impressions. How does your garden seem: thin or wide; big or small; long or short; boring or interesting, or simply 'okay'? The word you choose will tell you how you feel about the way the shape is working – 'interesting' suggests you quite like the way that you've dealt with an unusual shape: 'strange' obviously means you don't.

Levels

A steep incline is an opportunity to create something like a terrace or a rockery. A gentle slope can either be ignored or can be used (for raised beds, ponds, rockeries and so on).

The patio

- Is it in a sunny place?
  Is it big enough for general use without people having to spill over onto the lawn?
  Does water drain off it when it rains? Are all the paving slabs secure, or do they rock?

- Is it attractive? This is a question of its shape and what it's made of.

- The view from the patio is one of the most important you've got. Are you happy with it?

Paths, fences and walls

Are they doing the jobs they are supposed to and are they in good condition?

For instance, is the fence tall enough, and are the paths wide enough? Are there paths you don't ever use?

Common problems to look for include: wooden fence posts rotting from the bottom; split fence panels; cracked paths; uneven paving slabs that could be dangerous.

16

The lawn

A lawn should be *for* something rather than just be a space in between everything else. If it is meant to be beautiful – is it? If you want it both for your children to play on and to look nice – can they, and does it?

What about its condition? Is it mostly grass, or are there more bald patches, weeds and moss than anything else?

Note how much sun it gets and whether it drains well after rain. Does it crack in dry spells?

Finally, the lawn should be a pleasing shape and easy to mow.

17

Plants

Plants are a resource like any other. They have a value which you should try and assess.

Consider how much a plant contributes against how much space it takes. This is especially important for small gardens where space is limited, and where every plant must play an important part. In big gardens it is much less important – except where a plant is in a prominent position.

So something that is large and fairly uninteresting, apart from when it flowers, has less value than something with fine flowers, attractive leaves, and perhaps also good bark or stunning fruit. A lilac is lovely for three weeks in late spring, but apart from that is unspectacular. That isn't much value from a small tree. On the other hand, a crab apple *Malus floribunda* flowers brightly in spring, has an attractive shape and pretty, dark red fruit. It gives great value, and takes up less space.

Clearly this is subjective. You might love the smell of lilac – in which case, for you the value of a lilac is enormous!

When you assess the value of the plants in your garden, think in terms of shape, leaves, flowers, scent, bark and fruit.

Another important question is, does the plant do what it does on your side of the fence, or do the neighbours get the best of it? Again, if you miss the flowering of a particular plant because you always take holidays at the same time of year, is it worth keeping it however nice the neighbours say it looks?

Is it a good plant in the wrong position? For instance, if it flowers in winter, it should be visible from the house.

If you have just moved into a new house and don't know what something does throughout the year (and you don't want to wait) take a leaf and, if possible, a piece of stem to your local garden centre. They should be able to tell you about it. This will stop you removing plants that look boring during one season, but great at another. In winter you may not spot some herbaceous plants and bulbs. To find out about these, you'll just have to wait and watch!

Overhanging trees

The shade cast by these is an opportunity to grow interesting foliage plants which prefer these conditions.

Lime and sycamore, however, exude a sticky substance that discourages many plants. Only a few things can grow beneath them. Yew, horse chestnut and beech cast heavy shade and are very thirsty trees so little will grow beneath them too.

Other resources

Special features

Many gardens have other features – a pond, a stream,
a rockery, a greenhouse.

- Have you got something like this that you could make
  more of? It could be a small pond that, at present,
  looks out-of-place. You could remedy this with
  appropriate planting: things that move delicately in the
  wind and reflect well in water – bamboo, leycesteria
  or arum lily.

- Could the space be used better?
  Perhaps the pond is too small.
  Maybe you should remove it and
  use the space for a bed.

- Is there something that, with a little
  work, could become useful again?
  It might be a garden hut that is full
  of junk and needs clearing out. Or
  – and this is surprisingly common
  – a neglected compost heap that
  needs emptying.

Services

In any but the smallest plot, trailing a hose into the kitchen, or using watering cans, is a lot of bother. It is much easier to have a tap in the garden.

It is also convenient to have power outside. This is both for electrical tools (lawn mowers, drills, leaf choppers) and for powered features such as outdoor lighting and fountains.

Time

It is important to have an idea about how much time you want to spend on gardening because this will govern everything else.

Some kinds of gardening are intrinsically less time-consuming than others.

- An informal garden takes less time than a formal one.

- An ordinary lawn isn't very time-consuming but a fine one is.

- Mixed borders can look after themselves for most of the year – but vegetables, fruit and roses tend to be more demanding.

Money

Money spent on the garden is not wasted. Land is expensive and your garden is worth (and probably cost) a significant amount. As one of your assets, it makes sense to use it well rather than waste it. A fine looking garden, like a good kitchen or bathroom, adds value to the house.

SUMMARY

Once you understand, in a general way, exactly what you've got in your garden you will be better able to highlight its strengths and conceal its weaknesses.

To help you assess your own garden, these are the headings we use.

Your garden and its surroundings

Views from the garden
View from the house
Neighbours
Access
Light
Wind
Noise
Cats and squirrels

The structure of your garden

Size and shape
Levels
The patio
Paths, fences and walls
The lawn

Your resources

Plants
Overhanging trees
Special features (rockeries, ponds)
Services
Time and money

CHAPTER THREE

The Front Garden

The last two chapters are theory. To show how they work in practice we have applied them to a special case – the front garden.

Too many people treat the front garden as a back garden which just happens to be at the front of the house. It isn't – it's a special sort of garden, with its own needs, advantages and problems.

What should it be like?

What do you want?

Most of us want the same things from our front garden.

We pass through it several times every day. Unlike the back garden it is used day and night, summer and winter. So, it's important that it should be welcoming at all times.

It is also permanently on show. Guests, neighbours and strangers see it. For most people, making a good impression is therefore a high priority.

A front garden can also protect the house. This can range from blocking the view into the house, to preventing strangers from approaching it. So security is usually another consideration.

Some people use their front garden for parking a car. How big do you need to make this space?

If your house faces a busy road, you may want the front garden to shield the house from noise and dirt.

Many people keep their dustbins in the front garden – so you need somewhere to house them.

But this is not the place where you are likely to sunbathe, or barbeque, or let the children play. If you do plan to use your front garden for sunbathing or entertaining, it will affect every other decision you make.

All-year-round interest
This garden looks pretty in the spring and summer, but drab in the autumn and winter. Why not have some interest then as well?

24

Day and night interest
It is pleasant during the day, but not so interesting at night. What about some scented plants, especially night-scented ones?

Always on show
To look good, this garden requires constant work: the lawn needs cutting, weeding and feeding; the roses must be pruned, sprayed and dead-headed; the beds need weeding. Without maintenance, a garden like this looks tatty.

Conclusion
This garden works if the owner is able to do regular work, and doesn't mind how it looks other than during the day, in the spring and summer.

There are only certain people for whom that is sufficient. But for most others, a front garden like this is more a source of guilt and dissatisfaction than of pleasure.

What have you got?

Use the checklist in Chapter Two.

Size and shape
The front garden is usually the opposite of a back garden: a rectangle that is wider than it is long.

Does it seem interesting and pleasant, or dull and small?

It is usually small, sometimes so tiny there is hardly enough room for a pot.

Views
Seen from the street, is the front garden attractive?

Perhaps more important, does it flatter the house?

Is the view of the front garden from inside the house pleasing?

When you are indoors, do you see enough of the street outside – or too much?

Access
Is there a passage around the house to the back garden? This will make gardening the front easier.

How do the dustmen get to the dustbins? Make it difficult, and you're liable to end up with rubbish all over the place.

Conditions
How much sun does the front get?

You may have to deal with the wind because streets can be wind tunnels.

Is the soil in the bed nearest the house at all moist? The house often casts a big 'rain shadow', so this bed can be bone dry, even after rain.

Existing paths, fences and walls
Are the paths in the right place? If people tend not to

walk on them, the paths are in the wrong place.

Since it is likely that the paths will be used at night and in all conditions, are they safe?

Are the fences and walls in good condition and of the right height?

Existing plants

Have you anything really interesting in the front garden or are the plants relatively small, dull and insignificant? What's it like in winter?

Is there anything scented? Are there any plants climbing the walls?

Are there any large trees like poplars or willows near the house that could interfere with the foundations? If so, you might have to get rid of them. You may have to talk to the local Council about this, in case the trees are protected.

Lighting

A certain level of light in a front garden makes it safer, more welcoming and more secure.

If you are near a street light, it's probably not necessary to provide your own – but if you are not, it's worth considering.

Water

A tap near the front is a great help, both with watering and with washing the car.

Time

Even keen gardeners seem to prefer gardening in the back to gardening in the front. So when it comes to assessing how much time you are going to be able to give the front, don't be too optimistic.

Layout

This front garden is welcoming, safe and attractive. It doesn't need too much maintenance and it is interesting all year round.

Style

The front garden should work with the house rather than against it. A stark and formal garden (with box hedges, neat bedding and a topiarised privet hedge) would make a Victorian terraced house look severe. A decorative and informal garden might be nicer (a honeysuckle up the house, hellebores by the main path and a large winter flowering iris, *Iris unguicularis*, in the main bed).

Materials

The paving and fencing materials used in the garden should complement those used in the house, because the garden is always seen with the house in the background.

The lawn

A lawn is rarely of practical use. Few people encourage their children to play in the front garden. It takes up valuable planting space in what is normally a small area and requires regular maintenance to keep it looking good.

The path

The main path is wide and comfortable. A narrow front path is a nuisance, sometimes unsafe, and feels mean.

The car

If the car is parked in the front garden, you may want to arrange screening both from the house and from the road, unless, of course, you like looking at your car.

If the car is going to be in the front, are you going to wash it? The water that comes off the car shouldn't drain straight on to the beds. Ideally, it should go straight out into gutters in the road.

Walls

If you want to keep people from wandering up to the house but you aren't worried about security, low walls and high plants make a pleasant but quite effective barrier.

29

Large plants

Trees

Taller plants go well in a front garden because they fill the space between the house and the street.

But if the garden is small, a tree that casts a lot of shade is probably not suitable as it will make the rest of the garden dark and will rob the house of most of the light. This, of course, is the problem with the magnolias and cherries that are often in front of older houses. When they were first planted, they were small, delicate, flowering trees. It is only now that they have matured that they have become overpowering.

Tall, slim trees, or trees which don't have heavy leaf cover are often best for front gardens (see Charts in Chapter Eight, Framework Plants).

Climbers

These are great because they link the house and garden.

When you choose a climber, think about how you will support it.

Climbing roses need firm support – a trellis is best. Other plants can twine up something less formal like wire or drainpipes (clematis, wisteria, akebia, honeysuckle).

Some climbers are self-supporting (Virginia creeper and ivies). They are fine where the pointing is hard, but will damage an old wall with weak pointing.

Evergreen climbers are useful if the house wall is not attractive and you want it clothed in green all year round. Use an ivy or evergreen honeysuckle.

Shrubs

Shrubs are great in the front because they usually need little attention and are of a suitable size (between groundcover and trees). You can find shrubs that are interesting in all seasons (pieris, viburnum, cornus and so on).

Decorative plants

People tend to nibble at their front gardens: a small
plant here, a rock over there; a patch of this, a bit of that.
But as we've seen, this isn't the way to make a successful
front garden.

Be bold! Put some fine plants out there and some
vivid splashes of colour. The front will instantly look
more cheerful and more welcoming.

One of the features of a front garden is that you
normally walk through it along one path (from front
door to street). This means there are some parts you
see from a distance, and others you pass close up.

The parts you see in the distance should be bold,
with pleasing colours and a fine shape.

The areas you walk close to and see in more detail, should be planted more intricately. Bulbs and bedding plants would be suitable here. It's a good idea to leave gaps into which you can pop some bedding plants when necessary (when special guests come, or when the bed looks drab, or when you see something great in a garden centre).

In a front garden that is mostly stone and concrete use plant containers. The bigger, heavier ones are better as they are more difficult to steal. There are winter flowering bedding plants (universal pansies) that give colour all year round.

Scented plants, especially night-scented ones, add a lot to a front garden (night-scented stock is marvellous and tobacco plants are also good). Put them where you pass when you come in at night. Put aromatic plants by the main path, positioned so that you brush them as you pass.

If the front garden is very small, go for bold effects rather than subtle pastel schemes.

If it is tiny you won't have space for many plants. You are either going to have to find plants which give all year round interest (like *Pieris japonica* 'Variegata') or consider using a window box and containers. This will allow you to plant bright bedding plants all year round.

A certain amount of formality in a front garden is often suitable because the overpowering background – the house – is all straight lines and hard surfaces.

SUMMARY

Asking 'What is your garden for?' and 'What have you got?' frees you from the traditional solutions. We are not suggesting that you make a front garden like the one shown. Rather, we feel that you should ask yourself these questions and come up with your own solutions.

Back gardens present different opportunities and problems, so require different solutions.

CHAPTER FOUR

Layout

If you have discovered that your back garden needs reorganisation, launching yourself at it with a spade and barrowful of plants is fun, but often creates more confusion than when you began.

On the other hand, careful drawings which detail every plant, bed and stone don't feel like real gardening.

There is an Instant Gardening way between these two extremes.

The plan

All you really need to sort out when you are tackling the layout is the framework of the garden.

This is how the major features – the lawn, patio, paths, views and framework plants – work with each other and with the environment outside the garden.

Once the framework is right, everything else – beautiful plant associations, subtle colour co-ordination, interesting arrangements of foliage – is much easier, because all the other plants in the garden relate to it.

Example of how the framework affects layout

Imagine a small garden with, at one end, a big cherry tree that flowers spectacularly in spring.

You decide that what you most want from your garden is somewhere to enjoy the sun. But you don't want to spend much time or money gardening.

When you analyse what you've got you find that, although the garden faces south, it's shady in summer when the cherry is in leaf. You also have no real views, apart from that of the cherry. It is the only significant feature.

What is the best layout?

You could design the garden around your largest asset – the cherry tree. Being oriental, it might suggest an oriental style garden (bamboos, Japanese maples, etc). This sort of garden could win the admiration of your friends and even a garden prize. But you'd remain lily-white in summer. In fact, this scheme is designed more for the cherry than you.

The Instant Gardener would do something different. You want sun – and there isn't room for both you and the tree. You may be able to prune it, or move it but, if not, it has got to go. Without it, you'll get sun in summer. And who knows, while you are out sunbathing, you might feel like doing a bit of gardening.

Before you do anything to it, check to see what the garden would look like without it.

Imagine you find that it hid the view of a factory in the distance. If you had chopped down the tree, you'd have had to look at a chimney stack. Obviously, you'll need to put something in place of the cherry.

How about a smaller tree? Since summer sun is a high priority, you want one that isn't too dense when in leaf. If you haven't got a suitable specimen, go to your local garden centre and see what they've got. An amelanchier would be ideal (a small tree with white flowers in spring, delicate leaves and beautiful autumn colours).

So take a deep breath, cut down the cherry and plant the amelanchier. Under the cherry, where before there was only muddy lawn, you now have the perfect place for plants. How about bamboos to set off the amelanchier and perhaps a Japanese acer. A style is starting to emerge and the garden's beginning to look quite oriental (but, of course, minus the overbearing cherry).

So the Instant Gardening approach to layout – which doesn't really take a moment to do – has helped you alter the framework in such a way that you can build on the strengths (after all, your garden does get sun – even if at the moment the cherry hogs it) and conceal the weaknesses (the lack of space and the view of the factory).

Elements of the framework

When you are laying out a house, you wouldn't put the bath in the corridor. Bathrooms need to be near bedrooms because that fits in with how we live.

There are similar practical considerations that apply to laying out gardens. Putting the garden shed in front of your best view is clearly not sensible. What follows are some (we hope) less obvious observations about most of the main features in a garden. These are guidelines rather than rules.

Framework plants

These are the major specimens, and also those plants that are there for a purpose. They may hide an eyesore, maintain your privacy or just give borders height and shape.

If you need a new framework plant, decide what you want it to do and leave the choosing till later (or skip straight to Chapter Eight, Framework Plants).

If you already have some good beds or fine specimens, your layout should make the most of them. Be bold: if something boring hides a wonderful plant, move the boring one. If something is lovely but badly shaped, get in there with a pruning saw and secateurs.

The patio

The patio is the major bit of paving in the garden and if possible – even if you aren't totally happy with it – you want to avoid rebuilding it.

There are several Instant alternatives to rebuilding an unsatisfactory patio.

If it's too small, can you extend it? The most Instant way of doing this is using gravel with a brick surround.

If it doesn't get enough sun, can you increase the light it gets by pruning, or even by moving a tree; by painting surrounding walls white, or by developing another area of the garden as the sunbathing place?

If it is too big, it offers the perfect place to stand ornamental containers.

If one or two stones look bad, you can sometimes dig them up and use the holes for plants – aromatic plants are wonderful in these positions.

But if it is falling apart, or you don't like what it is made of, there may be no alternative to rebuilding it.

If you are going to rebuild the patio, remember that it is best near the house and connected to it by a good path. Staggering through the darkness with a tray of drinks over loose paving stones isn't healthy.

If you are going to have meals in the garden or entertain friends, access to the kitchen is also important.

Paths

Altering a path is one of the most Instant ways of changing the layout of a garden. This is because paths don't just get you from place to place, they also influence how the garden seems.

This effect is reinforced when the path runs between the lawn and beds and defines their shape.

There are alternatives.

Paths don't have to be put between the lawn and beds. If it makes the garden look better, bring the bed right up to the grass or put the path across the bed or lawn.

Stepping stones don't draw the eye in the same way as a solid path does. Use stepping stones to give access to the middle of beds, or as firm footing to cross a lawn, or where a more formal path would be ugly.

You could even do without paths altogether.

Another point is that paths that curve gently are more restful and pleasing than paths which wiggle busily.

Small lawns

Small lawns in small gardens are often more trouble than they're worth.

In a small garden, space is at a premium. Should you really give up a large part of your planting area for grass?

A small lawn needs to be in exceptional condition for it to look as good as a big one. Because you see them closer up, and look at them in more detail, weeds and bare patches are more noticeable.

Also the wear on a small lawn is concentrated, meaning more bare patches and more anxiety.

And for all but the smallest lawn you need a lawn mower and somewhere to store it.

There are alternatives to the small lawn.

If you need a sitting area, use paving or shingle. Shingle is hardwearing, quite attractive and very cheap and easy to lay.

If you need a play area, use forest bark. It is good for children because it is soft and they can fall safely on it.

If you don't need either, use the space for an extra bed.

Big lawns

Big lawns in big gardens make more sense.

A *big* expanse of green does look lovely and grass is a cost effective way of dealing with a large area. They also look good even if they aren't in excellent condition because you don't look at them in close up.

Note Whatever size the lawn, it shouldn't just be the area left over after the beds have been made. Make it a definite shape so that it looks good in its own right.

Water

Water features are quite easy to install and, though they cost quite a bit, add Instant appeal to any garden. Once established, they take little maintenance.

Water adds a special kind of magic to a garden. It looks wonderful, is a place to grow aquatic plants and it is ecologically fascinating: dragonflies, frogs, newts, snails and birds are all attracted to water. Finally, a fountain or cascade makes a pleasing and distracting sound.

Try to site any water feature in the light because light playing on water enhances it.

If you are concerned about young children falling into the pond, it's better not to have one. Making it 'out of bounds' or 'safe' will only result in domestic upset or worse, an accident and permanent guilt.

Try not to site a pond right under a large deciduous tree as you will have extra work keeping it clear of leaves.

Fountains are fun. They introduce height into a level garden. But watch out for splashing in windy positions.

You can have a water feature even in a small garden by growing aquatic plants in a half-barrel filled with water.

Rockeries

The fashion for rockeries comes and goes. But who cares? Done well, they add extra interest to any garden.

They look best in the sun partly because strong light shows up the rock well. Also many of the plants traditionally grown on rockeries prefer lots of sun.

The work area

Grouping the shed, compost heap, incinerator and place for storing the wheelbarrow in one area helps keep things relatively tidy and makes practical sense: you barrow rubbish to the heap, take the weeds out and put them in the fire, prop up the barrow ...

Sheds and tool stores
In the old days, a garden wasn't a garden without a garden shed. But as our plots get smaller, they are more difficult to justify. They take up a lot of space and are not usually things of beauty.

You can, with a little care, easily do without one. Many tools need only be stood out of the rain. There are waterproof outdoor cupboards where you can store the tools that need protection. The mower remains the problem but some modern mowers are relatively small and easy to store.

If you want a shed (they *are* useful for storing non-gardening things like bikes and toys) try to place it so that it isn't the focal point of the garden. If possible, put it in such a position that it can't be seen from the house (unless you have a wonderful, picturesque one).

The compost heap
Unless you are very tidy, a compost heap is always a bit of a mess, so it too should be in the work area.

Where space and waste are limited, use a compost bin.

LEVELS

The way the ground lies is part of the framework of the garden. What to do with slopes is a common problem.

Here is an easy way to think about slopes and levels.

If the ground slopes so much that earth is eroding, you should terrace.

If it slopes less than this, you can leave the slope as it is or you can decide to terrace it, depending on the effect you want.

If the ground is level, you have the option of making a slope or adding a terrace just to increase interest. But this does involve lots of heavy work.

Slopes

They give a garden a natural feel because in nature ground is seldom level.

They are much cheaper than terracing since you don't have to build walls.

They are great for children, who enjoy playing on them.

If your garden slopes away from the house, put progressively taller shrubs down the slope. This is an elegant and cheap way of seeing more garden.

Slopes that rise from the house are marvellous for displaying low flowers – such as bulbs – because you see the flowers at eye height.

A slope is the ideal basis for a rockery.

Sloping lawns used to be difficult to mow. Hover mowers have solved that problem.

Terraces

A wall made of stone looks lovely.

You get extra planting space in the raised (or sunken) bed.

You see plants from a dramatic angle – either up under them (beautiful for any shrub with pendulous flowers like laburnum) or on top of them (good for plants with foliage that forms an interesting mass like *Houttuynia cordata* 'Chamelion').

The vertical face of the wall can be a stunning planting space. Things that grow in, up and down it are set off by the stone.

There are, however, some other things to think about.

Terracing is most attractive when the garden rises away from the house because then you see the retaining wall. When the garden falls away you don't see the walls and the effect isn't so dramatic.

Moving earth and building walls is expensive in time or money.

Adventurous young children will use the terrace to play and jump from.

Beyond the garden

A garden is outside which means that things in the surroundings change the experience of being in it. Noise, views, wind – you can either take advantage of them or allow them to spoil your enjoyment. So it helps to think of what's around the garden as part of the framework.

BAD VIEWS
A bad view can become the focal point of a garden.

Screening
The obvious way of dealing with a grim view is to screen it. There are degrees of screening, ranging from partial through to complete. But, just as a bandage draws attention to the injury it covers, screening can draw attention to what it hides.

If you can shift the focus away from the bad view, it will need much less – if any – screening.

Changing the focus
Imagine that your neighbour has parked a caravan beside the fence and it looks horrible. You could try screening it with, for instance, a privet hedge, but everyone is going to wonder what is behind the hedge.

It's much more effective and Instant to change the focus of the garden. If you haven't an attractive, distant view, try planting something dramatic in a part of the garden away from the caravan. Work your layout so that it emphasises this specimen. Everyone will now look at the interesting feature and won't concentrate on the caravan. If you still need to screen it, you can now use a much less dense plant like a cut-leafed alder.

GOOD VIEWS

Making the most of a good view is one of the best,
cheapest and most Instant ways of improving any garden.
You can do it by framing or by sympathetic planting.

Sympathetic planting

Sympathetic planting brings a view into the garden.
Imagine there is a copse of big conifers some
distance away from your garden. Conifers in your
garden will make a visual link with the distant trees.
If you don't like conifers, you could use a plant that
is visually similar like a tamarix (a large shrub with
feathery foliage and
misty pink flowers).

Framing

You frame a view by drawing people's eyes in its
direction. Imagine that from your garden you can see
a baroque power station in the distance. You could
highlight it by planting shrubs either side of the view,
with a smaller shrub in the middle. The gap between
the tall shrubs will attract people's eyes to the
glorious building. But like a frame round a picture,
these plants should not be too eye-catching.

Cheating

One way of creating a good view is to donate a
plant to your neighbour. This is particularly effective
in small gardens that sit next to each other: the plant
forms a visual link between them and extends the
area of greenery. It's a fair deal – your neighbours
get a free plant, you get the use of their land. Give
them something that fits in with your garden scheme.

Night views

If you have night lights in the garden and good trees
nearby, direct some light onto them. Simply point
a couple of lights away from your garden. This has
a magical effect, providing your garden with a
backdrop of green.

LIGHT

You should work with and not against the light in your garden.

- Rockeries, lawns, most fruit, vegetables and herbs, aromatic and scented plants, ponds, fountains and cascades, look better in the sun.

- Other things work better in the shade: many foliage plants (such as epimedium and brunnera), some bog loving plants (such as primula and ligularia), woodland plants (rhododendrons, azaleas, camellias, ferns).

- But if an area is so shady that it's dark, you'll want to increase light levels. You could try painting nearby walls white or moving trees and other obstacles.

WIND

Scientific tests have established that hedges disrupt the wind for a significant distance downwind of themselves which creates a large area of calm. Walls don't – the wind simply rushes over them. So where wind is a problem, plant a hedge. They are also prettier than walls.

If your garden is quite windy, try planting things that move beautifully and sound interesting (some of the bamboos make an attractive noise and many of the willows move beautifully in a wind).

NOISE

You can reduce the impact of unpleasant noise with screening.

- A solid hedge will block quite a high level of noise.

- Even a single tree, if it is fairly big, will reduce the sound from nearby roads.

- A well-planted pergola over your sitting area can reduce the irritation of aircraft passing overhead.

If the unpleasant noise is not too loud, you can distract attention away from it.

- Many larger plants sound quite nice when they rustle in the wind. A few trees are especially delightful (*Populus tremula*, for instance, is great).

- Moving water (a cascade or fountain) makes a lovely noise.

- Do everything you can to attract birds to the garden: a pond draws many birds; put up a birdtable or birdfeeders; plant things that they like (cherries, pyracanthas, cotoneasters and other shrubs with berries).

Layout – some examples

By changing the layout, you can change the way most gardens seem. These are Instant Gardening solutions to some of the problems highlighted in 'What have you got?' (Chapter Two).

A NARROW GARDEN
Your garden seems narrow and you would like it to look broader.

Framework plants
Split the garden in two visually by putting something quite big half-way down it. This will make the area in front seem broader and tantalise the eye about what is behind.

- You could use a big plant. Since this will probably be visible all year round, it should be interesting in winter (you could use a silver birch or one of the bigger bamboos like *Arundinaria nitida*).

- You could also use something like a statue or large urn planted with bright bedding plants.

Paths and beds
Straight lines up and down a garden lead the eye directly to the end, which makes the garden seem narrower. Gentle curves will make it seem wider.

So the beds should bulge and the paths should meander.

The lawn
Stripes up and down the lawn will make the garden seem longer and narrower. Try different ways of mowing: diagonally; crossways; up-and-down and crossways (checkerboard), or doubling up the stripes. You could also remove the roller or use a hover mower.

A BROAD GARDEN
Your garden seems broad and you would like it to look longer.

Walls
In these gardens the end wall is usually overpowering. There are a number of things you can do.

- Use the wall in a positive way: grow a creeper up it; train a wall plant against it, or use the shelter it provides to grow something tender.

- Use tall shrubs to interrupt and soften the line made by the top of the wall.

- If there are overhanging trees on the other side, encourage a vigorous climber to grow into them.

- You can do all of these on one wall if it is long enough. Used well, it can be a real asset.

Paths
The paths in the garden could wind so that when you are on them, the width of the garden appears to be the length.

Views
If there are other gardens around you, extend the area of your garden visually by growing things that they have in their garden.

Patios
If you are going to build a patio, put it to one side of the garden, rather than across it. This will mean that, when you are sitting on it, the longest dimension – the width – will seem like the length.

View from the house
A semi-screening plant in the foreground of the main view from the house will improve it a lot. Branches and foliage close to the window prevent people seeing the whole garden all at once. Partly hidden, it will seem interesting and larger.

A SMALL GARDEN

One good reason a garden *seems* small is that it *is* small – and the temptation is to fill it with small plants. But when you step outside into the garden, your own proportions reveal how minute everything is.

Framework plants

It is much more interesting to burst the confines of the small space by adding the extra dimension of height. Plant one really tall, spectacular specimen.

But, since space is limited, it shouldn't cast too much shade or get too bulky. Because you'll mostly see it from quite close up, it should have fine features like lovely textured bark or very delicate leaves (*Prunus serrula*, for instance, has beautiful shiny bark and stays fairly narrow).

Decorative plants

Leave space for bedding plants. They provide wonderful instant colour all year round and since you haven't much space, you won't need to buy many which would be expensive.

Walls and fences

There's proportionally more wall area in a small garden than in a big one, so use the walls fully and have fun with them. Experiment with climbers, wall shrubs, hanging baskets, pots on the top, rock plants in the cracks and so on.

Views

Because the garden is small, make full use of any good view.

Containers

Plants in containers are a great asset. When they are at their best you can move them into prominent positions. Where a garden is so small that *you* can't move around *it*, you can get variety by moving the plants around instead. Have a few tall plants in containers to vary the height in the garden.

50

A BIG GARDEN

If you haven't got a gardener, or lots of free time and enormous energy and optimism, a large garden can be discouraging.

Framework plants

Put fast growing trees that don't need pruning or spraying near the end of the garden, for example birch or hawthorn.

You can split the garden into two: one part near the house is kept neat, tidy and colourful; the other, beyond, is left more to itself.

To separate the two, use shrubs rather than a fence or hedge. The shrubs won't stop people's eyes moving to the area behind and so preserve your greatest asset – the size of the garden. Some of these shrubs should grow to about 5ft high – things like mock orange and deutzia – others should be smaller.

Once you have control of one area, you can start spreading out into the wilderness. Or you might decide you prefer more wilderness and allow that to spread towards the house.

Other plants

When you buy plants, avoid those that demand work – like some roses (most of the hybrid teas and floribundas) and vegetables – and go for things that look after themselves like lavateras, potentillas or the old-fashioned shrub roses.

Lawn

A lawn works well in a big garden. If keeping it neat is too much work, plant bulbs in it, allow it to become longer and let weeds grow. That gives great Instant colour, makes the weeds look as if they ought to be there – they are, after all, just native wild plants – and cuts down on maintenance.

Employing a designer

If you don't want to do the layout yourself, these simple guidelines should get you a better result from a designer.

Tell the designer what you want from the garden and what you like and dislike in it at present.

Agree a rough budget. Try to avoid changing this halfway through the job because, once work has started, it is usually too late to make cost-effective changes.

If you are going to employ a contractor too, it is best to use a company that has both designers and contractors. Or find a designer who will oversee the work (see Chapter Five, which has a section on employing contractors).

SUMMARY

To improve a garden Instantly, it is usually enough to alter one or two parts of the framework – change the outline of a bed, plant a tree over here, move a couple of shrubs over there.

That first change will present you with new opportunities. You move a bush and suddenly see the border behind and the view beyond that would be improved by hiding the fence. Somehow the whole thing will start to work itself out.

Working this way round, your own style can emerge naturally. Instead of having to slavishly follow the rules of, say, the Italian garden, yours can look a bit Italian (and in another corner, perhaps a bit French, and somewhere else a bit oriental . . . whatever you want).

When you have decided what you want to do, you will be faced with a number of different jobs. What should you tackle first? Are there quick and easy ways of doing them?

CHAPTER FIVE

Hard Landscaping

These are the building jobs: making paths, walls, fences, changing levels etc. It is convenient to tackle them first – after all, it's easier to repair the fence and then fill the bed with flowers than to manoeuvre six-foot panels through an intricate planting scheme.

Physically, these jobs are some of the most demanding in the garden but there is an Instant way of approaching them.

To DIY or not to DIY

Doing the hard landscaping yourself seems to save money. Whether or not it does, and whether or not you should do it, is another matter.

Some jobs are easy enough for most people to do. Even without experience it is not very difficult to make paths, ponds and rockeries; lay small patios or put up a low fence.

But some jobs aren't easy. Unless you are skilled or keen, we believe that if you can afford it you should consider using specialists for laying anything but the smallest patios and for building retaining walls or brick walls of any length. They will make better use of the expensive materials and their skill should mean a better looking and more long-lasting result. You are saved a lot of hard work and the job will get done more quickly. The end of this chapter outlines how to approach employing contractors.

In this chapter we describe the easiest and quickest way of approaching hard landscaping jobs. Other, much more detailed books are devoted to the subject and we couldn't hope to better them. So for the more complex jobs refer to one of these books.

Fences

Replacing a fence, although easy to do, is relatively costly and time-consuming. The Instant Gardener avoids it if possible.

It is generally fairly easy to repair an existing fence. In a garden full of plants, people don't really notice the fence, so these repairs won't be too obvious.

Damaged panels

If parts of panels have cracked or fallen out, simply patch them.

If the damage is too extensive to patch, you can pull out the old panel and replace it with a new one. The new one will soon weather and blend in.

Low fences

A trellis fixed near the top will instantly give you extra height.

Rotten posts

When a post rots at its base, sink a new one beside it and bolt the two together.

Leaning fences

If the fence leans, large wooden struts wedged into the posts will bring it back upright. Once plants grow around the strut, it disappears.

Putting up a new fence

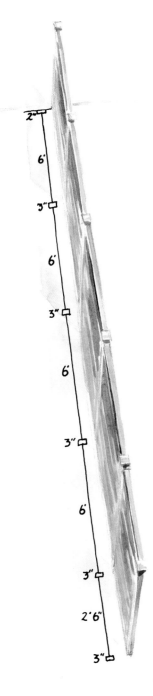

If the whole fence is falling apart, or if you are spending a lot of time propping and patching, then it may be easier to replace it.

This can be done on your own, but it is really a two-person job.

How many fence panels and posts you need

This is one of those things that seems simple until you face a pile of posts and panels at the retailers. With three panels, do you need three or four posts, remembering that you're starting at the house wall?

Measure the length to be fenced in feet and inches. Posts 3in wide are fine for panels up to 5ft high; it's better to use 4in posts for panels over 5 feet.

If the fence starts at a wall, you don't need a post on that wall. A 2in batten fixed to the wall is fine.

Sketch the fence on a piece of paper starting at a fixed end (such as a house wall). Virtually all fence panels are 6ft long.

Count the number of posts and panels!

If your garden isn't a convenient number of posts and panels (and when is it?), you'll have to shorten a panel. It's easy to do: simply take the battens off one end of the panel and fix them just inside where you are going to cut. The slats on many fence panels can be snipped with a pair of stout secateurs.

The height of the posts

If you are using post spikes, the posts can be the same height as the panels, but making them a couple of inches taller looks better.

If you use concrete, the posts should be about a third longer again than the amount above ground. So if you are going to have 5ft of post above ground, you need a 2ft hole, and a 7ft post.

You can secure fence posts with post spikes or concrete.

Post spikes
The advantages:

- They are less work than concrete.

- Transport back to and through your home is easier.

- You can fit panels as soon as the spikes are in, which makes the job quicker. This also reduces the need for careful measurements (and the chance of making a horrible mistake).

- If your fence has to cross an existing patio, there is a post-spike for fixing to concrete.

The disadvantages:

- Post spikes are more expensive than concrete.

- They tend to twist in stony ground. To minimise this use a 'dolly', a block with handles that goes onto the top of the spike. This will help you keep the spike correctly aligned as it goes in and prevents them being damaged as they are hammered. Dollies are sold by most retailers who stock post spikes.

- Rubble and big roots can stop the spike going in. You might have to resort to digging out the hole and using concrete.

Concrete
The advantages:

- You can do a perfect job, even in stony ground.

- The materials are cheaper.

The disadvantages:

- It is hard work: you have to move and mix ballast, sand and cement, and dig substantial holes.

- Most people let the concrete set before fixing the panels. This means the job takes at least two days. Some experts use a dry mix and put the panels in immediately.

- If you put all the posts in first and make a mistake with your measurements, it is hard to correct.

- You need longer posts.

Patios

Replacing a patio is a major job and one that is too often underestimated. It isn't just a matter of laying slabs of stone. The main work comes in the preparation – moving and disposing of what's there already; shifting heavy materials into the garden (cement and sand and paving slabs); sorting out the drainage; laying foundations. It's heavy work and it takes time, specialist tools and – if it is to be done well – specialist techniques. A middle-sized patio (say 18x12ft) with no special problems might take one person five full working days to lay properly. For a hobby gardener working solely at weekends that takes many weeks. That's weeks without a patio. Our Instant Gardening advice is – if possible, Don't Do It Yourself. If you do decide to DIY, allocate enough time for the job, try to get help, and refer to one of the recommended books.

Improving rather than replacing a patio is, however, relatively quick and easy.

- You can repair if it fits into the framework well but isn't in good condition.

- You should replace if it doesn't fit into the framework.

In other words, if it's in a sunny position but the pointing is bad or slabs have come loose or have cracked, you can simply repair it. If it is shaded by the neighbour's trees or overlooks the local abattoir, then it's a job for sledge hammer and skip.

- Repointing spruces up most paved surfaces. But it's hard on the back.

- If the shape is all right, but the surface is poor, you could lay a wooden surface or gravel.

- You can extend a small patio by using gravel surrounded by brick.

Paths

Because paths are so important to the way a garden seems, until you have settled on the best layout it doesn't make sense to lay them too permanently. It is best to try the path in one place (which will probably mean changing the layout of the lawn and the beds), live with it and, if necessary, change it.

To lay an Instant path simply cut a channel, put some sharp sand in as base and settle the stone.

Paths for different kinds of traffic can be different widths.

- Stepping stone paths need to be made of good-sized slabs.

- If the path is primarily ornamental and you aren't going to walk on it often, it need only be 1ft wide.

- If you are going to walk regularly on a path, or occasionally take a wheelbarrow along it, 1ft 6in will do.

- If you are likely to take a wheelbarrow down it often, it should be at least 2ft wide.

- If weeds in paths bother you, heavy duty plastic under the sand will deter them.

You may decide you don't need to lay your paths more formally. Or, once the layout seems right, you may want to use concrete and hardcore to make the path more secure and permanent (see booklist).

In general, most people use the same materials for both patio and paths. This isn't obligatory. Mixed materials – a gravel patio and brick paths – can look very good.

Terraces

It's easy to build a fairly low retaining wall (up to about 2ft). Build it with a slight backwards slope and in such a way that water can pass through – either dry stone or, if you use cement, leave plenty of drainage holes near the base of the wall. If water can't pass through the wall, it will build up in the retained soil and eventually the weight of liquid will force the wall over.

But it isn't at all straightforward to build a retaining wall over 2ft. At this height you need to take structural measures to stop it being pushed over by the weight of earth it's holding back. These measures vary for different soils and different sites. It's quite technical.

If you need to build such a high wall, check the booklist or contact a local builder who has experience of the conditions in your area.

A low retaining wall can be made out of all sorts of materials.

Railway sleepers

These make a marvellous wall which blends in with most gardens. They should only be used on straight runs.

Finding them is sometimes a problem. Try British Rail and builders' merchants. If you buy old ones, check that they aren't split or covered in oil, as this will ooze out in the sun. They are fairly costly and very heavy – which means it is hard work to transport and build with them. To cut them you need a chainsaw.

But walls made of railway sleepers are very robust and last a long time.

Log roll

These are split logs 8–12in high fixed to a roll of wire mesh. Log roll is widely available; the maximum rise you should make with it is 2ft. It's easy to handle, but doesn't make a very solid barrier.

Tree stakes

These are 3in diameter wooden stakes. You drive them in to hold back the soil. Quite cost effective, a terrace made of tree stakes is simple to build and looks natural. But it isn't very strong and will not prevent soil from eroding. The stakes might not last more than ten years.

Dry stone wall

A simple gardener's dry stone wall is made of stones piled in front of a bank of earth. Put the largest at the bottom – it should lean backwards at a slight angle. These walls are easy to build and look great because you can put plants between the slabs. But they don't usually last longer than five years because the earth behind shifts and the wall gradually collapses. They are, however, easy to repair.

You can make them out of all sorts of stone including broken paving, so they can be very cheap.

Rockeries

The chief attraction of a rockery should be the rocks. Ideally these should handsome enough to make the rockery look good even without plants.

A rockery is great Instant Gardening: get the right rock, place it well and you've got a wonderful feature.

Good rockery stones are large and heavy (usually there are only about ten to the ton). You will almost certainly need help getting them in place and putting them into the rockery. Where access or carrying is an insuperable problem, use the lightweight 'Tufa' stone.

You can usually get rockery stone from garden suppliers. Before you buy, try to go and look at what's on offer. Choose the individual stones. The supplier will normally deliver for you.

Each stone has its own shape, surfaces and character. When you make the rockery, take a little care about how you arrange the stones. The effect you are after is a miniature rocky landscape: several close together can look as though a big stone has been split; an upright stone can create the look of a crag and so on.

If you haven't much stone, make one small area a 'rock feature'. Pile the stones together into a rocky mound. If this rises higher than the surrounding bed, you can then use the rock feature as part of a change of level which will increase interest. If instead of this you space the stones widely, they will gradually get overwhelmed by plants and disappear from view.

Which brings us to rockeries made of rubble. These seem like a good idea. In practice, they rarely work. As rubble isn't attractive, most people end up trying to hide it with plants. The result is a sloping bed with bits of rubble peeping through.

If your site is level, it is easy to build a rockery and pond at the same time because the earth you excavate to form the pond goes into the mound that forms the basis of the rockery.

Rockery plants

Many traditional gardening books assume that you are
going to grow alpine plants on a rockery. These lovely
little plants hate being waterlogged. To grow them
successfully, add gravel to the soil and pay particular
attention to drainage. They also need lots of sun.

But you don't have to grow alpines on a rockery. If,
for instance, you like rockeries but your garden is
wet, or shady – and therefore unsuitable for most
alpines – don't grow them. Instead, use other small
plants that like damp conditions: dwarf bamboos,
ajugas, astilbes, primulas and so on. These look
marvellous against rock and make an unusual and
interesting feature.

You can, of course, grow alpines without building a
rockery. Add stone chippings to the surface of a
well-drained bed in a sunny position. One or two big
rocks will turn this into an attractive feature that is
half-way to being a rockery.

Ponds

A pond is a wonderful Instant feature. It is relatively easy to make and looks good immediately, even before the plants have established themselves.

There are two sorts of pond – sunken and raised.

- A sunken pond is easy to make and fairly cheap.

- A raised pond is a container (usually made of brick or stone) filled with water. It looks rather formal and works best near a patio where you can build the surround from similar stone.

Both must be lined with waterproof material.

Plastic or butyl liners

These are sheets of waterproof material. Lightweight and easy to transport and work with, they fit any shape and make natural looking ponds.

If possible get a good quality butyl liner rather than a thin, cheap polythene one (see Pond warning!). The best are quite expensive but are covered by a long guarantee.

Liners come in standard measurements (10x6ft, 12x8ft etc). You need one that is about 3ft more than the maximum length and breadth of your pond, so that you have enough for the depth, with some left over to make the edges secure. If the pond is going to be very deep, you obviously need a bigger liner.

Premoulded shapes

These are robust and easy to work with and need little preparation. But they are clumsy to move around – particularly for large shapes. Think about access and transport *before* you get one.

Concrete

We don't recommend using concrete to make a pond. Although it is cheap, you have to lay it on a very solid foundation. If it does crack and leak (which is quite likely), it is difficult to repair.

Depth

If the edges are shallow, more wildlife can get into (and out of) the water.

Some part should be at least 2ft deep so you can grow water lilies and oxygenating plants (which are essential if you want to keep fish).

A flat shelf 9in below the surface allows you to grow plants that like being partly submerged. They'll help hide any exposed liner at the edge.

Making a pond with a liner

Preparation is vital. Once you've dug the hole, remove any obvious stones. Then cover the exposed earth with at least a couple of inches of sand, wet newspaper or old carpet. This will prevent the liner from being pierced by stones that work their way through as everything settles.

To fit the liner, put it over the hole with weights on the edges. Fill with water. It stretches until it fits the hole.

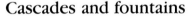

Cascades and fountains

Both need electricity. Organise this before you buy them. They are surprisingly straightforward to install.

Pond warning!

When you make a pond try to get it right first time. If you do, maintenance is easy (just the occasional cleaning, tending to the water plants etc). If you don't, you're in trouble. To repair a leaking pond you've got to drain it, save the water plants and fish, find and plug the leak and dry out soggy patches of garden.

Rubbish

When you do hard landscaping, it's inevitable that there'll be stuff to get rid of – bits of wood, clay, rubble.

You can sneak small amounts into your domestic dustbins, but most dustmen notice and object to these things. Money sometimes helps.

If you have more than a couple of big bags of rubbish it makes sense to go to the Council tip where you can dump it for free. Check the opening times; they can be eccentric. Use heavy duty bags which you can buy from builders' merchants. Though they are more expensive than domestic plastic bags, they save having to scrape clay and rubble out of the car. If you take a bit of care, you can re-use them.

If you've got a lot of rubbish, consider hiring a skip.

Skip hire companies are in Yellow Pages under 'Waste Disposal'. Skips come in a variety of volumes from mini to large. The ends of some flip down which makes for easier filling at first. These are called 'front loaders'.

You'll need a skip licence if it stands in the road. Phone your local Council to check the formalities – mostly you get the licence from the Engineers' Department and they are often free.

You have to pay for the skip on delivery. Ask the hirer to include some lights to hang on your skip, since you are legally responsible for lighting it at night.

On the day of delivery, if it is going to be parked in the road, reserve a place for it, otherwise you could have to haul your rubbish quite a way because the skip driver will not wait for the right space to come free.

Employing contractors

Employing contractors is rarely fun – they are, after all, strangers in your territory – but there are ways of making the experience less painful.

- The best way to find a contractor is through recommendation, either from friends or a retail outlet that you trust.

  If you can't find anyone this way, ask to speak to former customers of any prospective contractor.

- Know what you want done, tell them clearly and make sure they understand. A lot of problems come from poor communication between client and contractor.

- Try to get quotes from more than one firm. Ask also for an idea of how long each phase of the job will take. Compare the quotes and schedules – they should tell you how different firms view the job.

- Try to agree a finish date. And anticipate that, in all but extraordinary cases, they'll finish late.

- Only employ a firm where you can communicate with someone in a responsible position, preferably someone who is going to be on site.

- Try to keep an eye on work as it is done (liaise with the person you get on with). Don't let things drift. This is where a schedule comes in useful.

- It is reasonable to pay up to a third of the cost at the beginning of the job.

- Never pay the whole sum before completion or the job may never be finished.

- Landscape gardening is hard work. Supply lots of tea and biscuits. If nothing else, it generates good will.

- Delicate plants will get trampled on. Move them rather than get angry.

SUMMARY

Some garden books make hard landscaping seem so simple. A couple of paragraphs ('Level the site. Then, having put in adequate drainage . . .') and a picture of a hand holding a trowel loaded with cement could tempt you into trying to do something that takes days and days of backbreaking labour. And the end result often isn't that impressive.

We aren't saying that you shouldn't do hard landscaping. It's just that we believe that there are easier, more Instant ways of doing some things, and harder ways that might well be better done by professionals. As long as you know the difference, and know what you are letting yourself in for, you can't go too far wrong.

Another thing to consider is – do you want to spend your precious leisure time building rather than gardening? Perhaps so – but again, that should be your choice, rather than the result of being trapped in a big job you can't seem to finish.

CHAPTER SIX

Soil

Traditional gardening equates hard work on the soil with virtue. The impression has been given that only by digging, preferably double digging, can you improve it. Instant Gardening doesn't encourage this form of virtue – although it is true that if you do some work on the soil, everything that grows in it will benefit.

Soil is divided into layers. Topsoil feeds the plants: it should be rich and open and at least 4in thick. Subsoil should drain well and contain some nutrients. Unless there is a specific reason for it (or unless you actually enjoy digging), don't mix the two. At last, a reason to avoid heavy digging!

For most gardens the best thing you can do – and it is little effort and has an almost Instant effect – is to work a couple of inches of well-rotted manure into the topsoil in the autumn.

But some soils do have problems which need more attention.

Low fertility

If the soil looks dusty and your plants don't grow very well, your soil is exhausted. If weeds don't grow where there's bare earth, this confirms it. The soil in many old urban gardens is relatively worn out.

You could try and improve the fertility with chemicals, but this will have only a very short-term effect. What the soil really needs is both better structure and better composition.

The best treatment is simply to add plenty of well-rotted manure – which can done in these soils at any time of year. Begin by working it in around the bigger plants.

You could also add organic fertilisers such as 'hoof and horn', bonemeal, fish, blood and bone, and seaweed. These release their nutrients slowly and contain a wide range of minerals and trace elements.

Lack of topsoil

If your plants don't grow well and when you dig in the soil there is no distinct top layer, you lack topsoil. In these cases it is not enough just to add manure.

If the garden is small, it isn't that expensive to buy topsoil. Most garden retailers sell it, either in bags or loose for larger loads. Check it doesn't contain big lumps or lots of clay – some commercial topsoil is more like rubble. You need enough to spread about four inches in depth.

Before you spread the topsoil, dig organic matter into the subsoil.

For bigger gardens, buying topsoil is usually prohibitively expensive. In this case just improve the soil around each major plant with compost and bonemeal and add manure each autumn (see Planting, Chapter Eleven). If possible add compost to the soil every autumn (big gardens generate lots of lovely stuff for composting). The soil will improve bit by bit.

Soils that drain slowly

If water doesn't drain away freely after it rains and the soil cracks in dry spells, it means the earth contains lots of clay or is very compacted. Plants probably won't grow well in these conditions – although moss will. Compaction causes a lot of problems for lawns.

There are no Instant solutions to this problem because you've got to open up the subsoil. Remove the topsoil and dig gravel or grit into the top 10ins or so of the subsoil. With subsoil that contains clay, gypsum, 'Claybreak' or 'Landspeed' will help.

You should also add organic matter to the subsoil. Use something coarse like mushroom compost, forest bark, or compost from the heap. Peat isn't much use as it is too fine and soon gets washed away. Use plenty of it – within limits, the more you add, the more likely it is you'll overcome the problem.

When you return the topsoil, add manure to improve it too.

Another (relatively expensive and difficult) solution is to lay land drains. Consult the booklist, or a firm of expert landscape gardeners.

The battle against these conditions is tough and not at all Instant. You might decide to garden with them. Some plants can deal with bad drainage. Try willows or dog-woods. These send down strong tap roots and will dry quite large areas around them. You can experiment with moisture-loving plants like hostas (low spreading plants with magnificent leaves which come in a range of colours from grey through to stunning green and gold variegations).

Soils that drain too fast

If the soil is sandy and dry and your plants look weedy, your soil doesn't hold water for long enough. The problem with these soils is both drought and lack of goodness because, as the water rushes away, it dissolves out the nutrients.

The best way to improve them is to add organic matter. Use mushroom compost or our old favourite, well-rotted manure.

Some plants thrive in these soils. They include: herbs like lavender, rosemary, bay and thyme; ornamental plants with grey foliage like teucrium, caryopteris; and plants that originated in countries with a hot climate – nicotiana, cistus, geranium, cotinus, cerastostigma.

Acidity and alkalinity

Acidity and alkalinity (the 'pH') of soil is a favourite subject with academics, authors and manufacturers of soil testing kits. Most gardeners simply garden and do perfectly well without bothering about the 'pH'.

But it is worth noting:

- Some plants need acid soils. These are called 'ericaceous' plants and include all the rhododendrons, azaleas, pieris and camellias. There are others – if in doubt, ask at a garden centre.

- Some soils are naturally acid – if rhododendrons thrive in your area, the soil is probably acid. Other soils are naturally alkali (they contain lime or chalk) and ericaceous plants won't grow in them.

If you want ericaceous plants and have unsuitable soil, put them in plenty of ericaceous compost. Don't invest in large numbers of specimens – put them in one or two at a time and see how they do.

Although mushroom compost is a fantastic soil conditioner, it is alkaline and is not suitable for ericaceous plants.

Soil testing kits establish the acidity or alkalinity of the soil in a particular place. But across even a small garden the soil can vary greatly and, to be sure you understand it, you have to take a series of tests across the whole garden. This is only worth doing if you become very interested in the 'pH' of soil.

Compost heaps

Compost heaps provide wonderful organic matter. We describe how to make a simple one in Chapter Fourteen.

Peat

For some time, people have been spreading peat all around the garden as a soil conditioner. Unfortunately it is not very effective: it is too fine to condition the soil for long and contains no nutrients.

Also, extracting peat for use in gardens is ruining rare and beautiful natural habitats.

For soil conditioning it's better to use compost from the heap, manure and, for anything but ericaceous plants, mushroom compost.

SUMMARY

Most garden plants take much more from the soil than they give back. If previous gardeners have done nothing about it, the soil in your garden will have been getting poorer for many decades.

There is no Instant one-off treatment that can totally remedy neglect like this. But even after the first treatment, you'll be able to see the improvement: seeds will germinate better; plants will start to grow more strongly and flowers will be bigger and brighter.

Working the soil will also be more fun. It will be easier to dig and there'll be more life in it – it will even smell better. As worms flourish, you will attract more birds. And soon those bare patches of exhausted soil will be smothered in a glorious growth of healthy weeds.

CHAPTER SEVEN

The Lawn

When you first make a garden, the lawn seems like Instant Gardening. You just lay a bit of turf on the earth and hey presto! living lino.

But as those of us who have a lawn know, once you've got it, it isn't Instant at all. You mow, feed, spike and weed it and everyone else's grass still seems greener.

It needn't be like this.

Broadly speaking, there are two kinds of lawns: ornamental and utility.

The first is beautiful. To look good it needs lots of work, throughout the spring, summer and autumn, for many years. It should only be used occasionally – and not at all by children and dogs.

The utility lawn is more robust but not so attractive. It is not so demanding and stands more use.

For many of us the problem is that we want the impossible: an ornamental lawn which only gets attention occasionally and which doubles up as a football pitch at weekends.

The best way of improving your lawn is to be realistic. If it is a utility lawn, don't aim for perfection. If it is to be a superb-looking ornamental lawn, protect it and be prepared to put a lot of work into it.

CHANGING THE LAWN

For an excellent lawn you need good drainage, soil free of big stones and a top layer of fine, rich soil. Most of us inherit our lawn from previous owners. Most of them didn't go to the expense and bother of laying land drains or of clearing the soil of big stones. So, unless you are going to do all that yourself, you may have to settle for what you've got.

But, if you're prepared to work, it is possible to change an existing lawn. To do this you must alter the balance between the fine and coarse grasses.

To make it more ornamental

Utility lawns contain hardwearing 'rye' grasses, ornamental lawns don't. To make a utility lawn more ornamental, you have to discourage the rye grasses.

Regular, frequent mowing with low blades tips the balance in favour of the finer grasses.

If you start cutting like this, remember to feed frequently since a lot of nutrition is being taken out of the lawn.

To make it more hardwearing

If the lawn is being damaged by overuse, let it grow longer and mow less frequently. The coarser, more hard-wearing ryes will overwhelm the finer grasses.

The meadow

If your lawn is weedy, you might decide to aim for a mixed, or meadow-like lawn.

All it needs is a poor soil (not usually a problem in an urban garden). Plant bulbs and wild flowers in the lawn. Don't go into the country and dig up wild flowers. Buy a packet of wild flower seeds, germinate them and bring them on in pots, then plant them out.

If you want spring flowers, leave the first cut till July; if you want summer flowers, mow up to June, leave it, then begin mowing again in September.

These lawns are forgiving, hardwearing, good for birds, rather messy and attractive. They work better as a large lawn where you can also leave one area longer than the rest.

Other problems

Bad drainage

One reason a lawn gets soggy is that, when people walk on it, they compact the soil.

Apart from remaking the lawn, the only way to deal with this is by aeration. Make deep holes in the lawn with a fork; there are special tools for the job but the ones on the market are not very good. Only aerate when the lawn is dry. But be warned: aerating a lawn is hard, physical work.

To really pamper a lawn, aerate it, apply and rake in a top dressing of horticultural sharp sand and soil-less compost. The compost adds goodness and the sand helps the drainage.

Moss

Small areas of moss here and there aren't really a problem. But although moss looks nice and green in wet weather, it isn't hardwearing and quickly goes brown when it gets dry.

With a real problem, it's more effective to change the conditions to discourage moss rather than applying moss killer (which is just a short term solution). Moss thrives in poor drainage and acid soil. So aerate the lawn and, if the soil is acid, add lime. Lawn sand in autumn also helps. When you do the last cut in winter, leave the grass slightly long. This is because moss continues to grow into winter and can overwhelm very short grass.

Shade

Grass likes plenty of sun and doesn't really thrive in the shade. You can get seed mixes specifically designed for shade – but if your lawn is suffering because there isn't enough light, it's better to question whether it should be there at all.

Re-laying a lawn

If your lawn is mostly bare or has more weed than grass, it may be easier to re-lay it rather than nurse it back to health.

Making a lawn takes quite a bit of work but, given luck with the weather, you should be able to do an area about 20x10ft in a weekend. If the soil drains really badly you'll have to lay land drains which is a major job (see booklist).

You can lay a lawn anytime from spring to autumn but not in a heatwave or a very cold or wet spell.

Choosing the right grass

Choose a grass which promises the right balance between looks and durability. This is not the time for optimism. If the grass is not tough enough and the children wear it bald, you'll have wasted time and money and, in addition, you will have more domestic strife. Equally, try not to err too far on the side of caution or your lawn will never look good enough. New seed mixes have narrowed the gap so that the lawns they produce are better looking, tougher and need less work.

TURF
The advantages

- You can walk on it as soon as it is laid (give it three or four weeks before using heavily).

- Laying turf is straightforward.

The disadvantages

- Turf costs more than seed.

- Delivery needs to be organised.

- You should lay turf as soon as it comes because it spoils quickly.

- Quality can be a problem.

SEED
The advantages

- You can get a specific mix of grasses including some for shade.

- With seed you get assured quality.

- Seed is cheap and light.

The disadvantages

- Getting even distribution and good germination requires care and skill.

- You have to protect the seed from birds.

- It needs constant watering.

- It takes months to get established.

Laying a lawn

This is quite hard physical work because turf is surprisingly heavy stuff. But if you are prepared for that, it is a job that is well within the range of most gardeners.

- Clear the site back to the topsoil.

- If the soil doesn't drain well, remove the topsoil and put to one side.

- The top of the subsoil should be at least 4in below the surface of the new lawn. Get rid of any excess.

- Improve the subsoil with gravel and mushroom compost (which, being alkaline, will help reduce moss). This will open the subsoil and improve the drainage.

- Using a rake, level the subsoil.

- Compact the subsoil by walking on it.

- Improve the topsoil by removing any large stones. Mix in fine organic matter (leafmould, mushroom compost, sedge peat). There should be sufficient to spread at least 2in over the whole surface.

- Return the topsoil and rake it carefully to remove stones.

- Add and mix in a handful of bonemeal per square yard.

- Level the site.

- Compact again by walking on it with your heels or use a roller.

- Rake again to create a fine surface.

Don't lay the lawn when the soil is wet. As you walk on wet soil you compact it and so you'll be starting your new lawn at a disadvantage.

Laying turf

Most of the work is done once you've finished the preparation.

- When you lay turves, do it so that each rectangle of turf bridges the gap between the rectangles in the row before (like brickwork).

- Fill the gaps with earth.

- It is a good idea to lay a sturdy board like a scaffold board across several turves and stamp on it. This levels and settles the turf.

- Water thoroughly every day. A light sprinkling is not enough, water must reach the soil beneath the turf.

Sowing seed

- To get even distribution, bulk up the seed with seed compost and divide the mix into two. Spread one lot (by hand, as in medieval pictures) going up and down. Spread the other pile going from side to side.

- Wind black cotton between short stakes to protect the seeds from birds. Fine ribbons of silver paper tied to the stakes also help.

- Water the new lawn lightly once a day. Heavy watering will flood the seedlings and even a short period of drought will kill them.

- Wait until the grass is 3in long before you first cut it. Don't start to use it for at least a month after that.

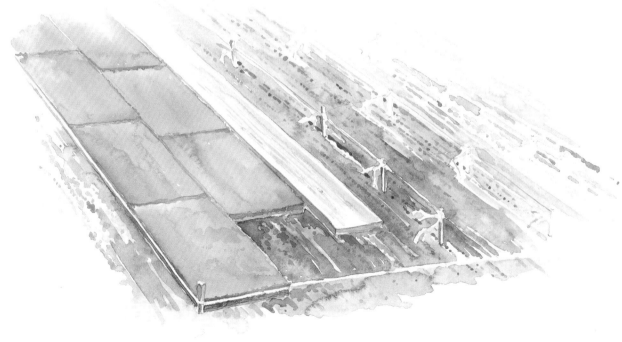

Buying Turf

Turf should be as fresh as possible. The ideal arrangement is for the retailer to organise delivery straight from the turf farm to your house.

Where this isn't practical, inspect the batch you are buying. It should be green – yellowing is a sure sign that it isn't fresh. Unless you specifically want a meadow-like lawn, check that there are no weeds in it. The turves should be of a relatively consistent thickness: if they vary a great deal you'll have to put earth under them to get any sort of level. The soil shouldn't contain big stones.

If you must store turf, keep it in the shade and don't let it dry out. Storing more than two days is asking for trouble.

Turf comes in different grades. Starting with the least expensive, these are:

Untreated Meadow Grass
Coarse grass with weeds in it. Okay for the largest areas or a wild garden.

Treated Meadow Grass
Coarse grass without weeds. Hardwearing but of variable quality.

Other Turf
Turf for growing in shade, or seeded with wildflowers, is becoming more widely available than in the past.

Cumberland
The finest – inappropriate for anything but bowling greens.

Cultivated
Purpose-sown grass, generally of a specified mix. Good quality, looks nice, costs more.

Seed

The most hardwearing is usually described as 'for sports', while the finest is described in different ways: 'superfine' or 'ornamental'.

There's a grass called 'Quicklawn' which germinates fast and takes less time to knit together. There are also several mixes specifically for shady areas, and you can get meadow mixes with wildflower seed included.

SUMMARY

Try not to let the lawn become the focus for dissatisfaction and guilt.

- If it doesn't look right, try altering how you look after it.

- If it takes too much work, are you expecting too much from it?

- If you expect too much from it or if it is beyond repair – how about re-laying it?

- Or you may decide that you don't really want a lawn at all.

CHAPTER EIGHT

Framework Plants

Suppose you need a new framework plant in one corner of your garden. The only trouble is, you aren't confident that you know enough about horticulture to choose the right one. Or perhaps you have finally lost patience with a big shrub that darkens your living room. It has to go. Dare you do it?

Although these seem like difficult problems, dealing with framework plants is really quite easy.

Choosing framework plants

Take the example of framework plant which is to go half-way down a long narrow garden.

Since this plant forms part of the main view of the garden it should look good all year round. The obvious solution is a large evergreen. Although these are expensive, you can get small fast-growing conifers like *Cupressocyparis leylandii* or large leafed evergreens like laurel quite cheaply. These will quickly get up to the required size.

But for a prominent position like this a framework plant should be interesting – especially in winter, when the rest of the garden is at its dullest. So these trees, both unvarying green all year, aren't such a good idea.

What you are looking for is something a bit special. It doesn't need to be that spectacular in summer when everything else is at its best.

So the choice of plant isn't a difficult one. There aren't hundreds that fit the bill.

You also know the conditions – light, soil and water – of the new framework plant's home. Remember, the plant that loves shade will not thrive in bright, hot sun and something that is described as a sun lover will hate a shady position.

Furthermore, the new framework plant will have to co-exist with your existing garden.

Imagine you have a pleasant, mature, natural garden. Around the edges are good-looking, dense trees (hawthorns, a plum, ashes and, in the distance, horse chestnut and sycamore). There are bluebells in spring, bulbs and weeds in the lawn, large shrubs like lilac and mock orange (philadelphus – white flowers in summer) and plenty of pretty summer herbaceous plants (foxgloves, delphiniums, lupins).

Unfortunately one of the trees in a sunny border was damaged in a storm and has died. You are now overlooked by your neighbours.

So you need a new framework plant. You know what it's got to do and you know the shape and size you need.

There aren't that many possibilities. Imagine your local garden centre stocks two trees that you like: a golden false acacia *Robinia pseudoacacia* 'Frisia' (a golden leafed tree with a bold shape) and a mountain ash *Sorbus aucuparia* (coarse feathery foliage, red berries in autumn and fine autumn colours).

These would have opposite effects on your existing garden.

The golden false acacia, being so brightly coloured, would become the focus of the garden. Everything else would start to look a bit drab.

But the mountain ash would complement everything else in the garden. It would settle in nicely, adding a number of interesting features (berries and autumn colours) without disturbing what you've already got.

So choosing the false acacia would allow you – almost encourage you – to introduce other plants with strong colours and powerful shapes. Unless you are really bored with your existing garden, it makes sense to go for the mountain ash.

But imagine you have just moved into a house with a small garden. It is packed with all too familiar plants which you find boring: irises, asters, wallflowers, a pyracantha, and an old laurel.

One obvious way of changing this is by introducing a powerful framework plant. In this case you are looking for something which is going to liven up the garden and make it look more fun. A golden leafed acacia would be an excellent choice.

The bright yellow leaves of the acacia give you the opportunity to start making an exciting garden. Using the existing plants almost as a back-ground, you could introduce other exciting plants (for a start, *Choisya* 'Sundance' would work brilliantly with its golden evergreen foliage).

So thinking about the effect of a new framework plant on your existing garden narrows down your choices even further.

Removing framework plants

Before you get rid of any large plant, check to see whether it is not a framework plant which is doing an important job in the garden. Of course, in smaller gardens, even quite small shrubs can be framework plants.

If it is a framework plant, sort out what is going to do its job *before* you dig it up. This may sound obvious, but too many people do something irrevocable and then suffer the consequences for years.

Say you don't like a large forsythia that dominates one of your beds.

You check to see what it does and you discover that the wall behind is made of ugly brick with bad pointing. If you remove the shrub, you'll have to do something about the wall.

What can you do?

Replace it
Finding a replacement of the same size might be expensive.

Improve it
Forsythia is only interesting for a couple of weeks in spring when it flowers. So a summer-flowering climber would vastly increase its value. *Clematis viticella*, for instance, flowers in late summer. Growing this up your forsythia means you get a burst of yellow in the spring and lovely purple flowers in late summer. If you haven't the bed space, plant the climber in a pot.

Be tough with it
After flowering in spring, cut it back hard and put bedding plants in the space around the base that you've just created. But it is very vigorous and will soon be a problem again.

Grow a replacement
The trick is to put something fast-growing in near the forsythia. By limiting the spread of the forsythia and encouraging the new plant you will soon be able to get rid of the forsythia completely. *Lavatera olbia* 'Rosea', for instance, would be a good alternative. It is a vigorous shrub that flowers from May to October with pink flowers.

Hedges

A hedge should not just be a green wall with the disadvantage of needing a regular trim. There are several ways of making a dull hedge look more exciting.

- If it is informal, treat it as a frame for other plants like honeysuckle or clematis.

- Use it as a background to display something colourful: put a gold-leafed berberis against a privet hedge: or white-stemmed *Rubus cockburnianus* against a dark conifer hedge.

- Replace hedge plants at intervals with small trees or hedge shrubs with different foliage: for instance, replace an ordinary privet every couple of yards with a golden one.

- Cut it into interesting shapes (topiary). This is a surprisingly Instant technique, especially with a misshapen hedge – that is, one that isn't rectangular. Trim to take advantage of the irregularities: a high portion becomes a hump; a low place is a dip; a point becomes the head – and suddenly you've got a Loch Ness monster. A topiarized hedge doesn't even need to look like anything in particular, but can simply be an abstract shape.

New hedges

If you are thinking of making or replacing a hedge, consider using slow growing plants. Although vigorous plants like *Cupressocyparis leylandii* seem like a good Instant solution, being fast-growing, you will need to trim them regularly. This becomes very time-consuming when they grow taller.

Another problem is that very fast-growing plants like these will starve and dry out even quite a large border: a hedge is, after all, just a number of fairly big shrubs growing close together in a straight line.

A slow-growing hedge demands less of the soil and has the added advantage of needing less clipping (with all the collecting and burning or composting associated with that job). If you go for a slow-growing hedge, it may well be worth spending extra on bigger specimens so that it gets established more quickly.

SUMMARY

Choosing specimens for the framework is quite easy. All you have to do is fit the right plant to the situation.

The charts that follow describe a few of the more commonly available plants. Many wonderful plants are not mentioned. However, thinking like this – in terms of advantages and disadvantages – is a great way of choosing any plant.

Trees (Figures for height apply to specimens originally 5ft high)

Name	Good Points	Disadvantages	Vital Statistics
Acer capillipes Snake-bark Maple	Wonderful striped bark. Red in autumn.	Slightly unnatural shape. Not easy to find.	In 3yrs about 8ft. Casts medium shade.
A. griseum Peeling-bark Maple	Weird peeling bark. Leaves go stunning scarlet in autumn.	Expensive. Can take years for the bark to peel.	In 3yrs about 6ft. Casts light shade.
A. negundo 'Flamingo'	Good for semi-screening. Fine white, pink and green leaves. Moves well in a breeze.	Not very hardy. Hates strong winds.	In 3yrs about 8ft. Casts light shade.
A. palmatum	Lovely cut foliage. Red or orange in autumn.	Expensive. Burns in hot sun or wind.	In 3yrs about 6ft. Casts light shade.
A. palmatum 'Crimson Queen'	Eye-catching crimson foliage. Good summer screening.	Looks gloomy in shade. Ugly in winter.	In 3yrs about 8ft. Casts light shade.
Alnus glutinosa 'Imperialis' Cut-leafed Alder	Delicate, finely cut foliage. Moves well in wind and makes a pleasant noise.	Late to come into leaf. Can be difficult to obtain.	In 3yrs about 8ft. Casts heavy shade.
Amelanchier	Pretty white flowers in spring. Beautiful red/orange autumn colour.	Can be damaged by late frosts.	In 3yrs about 7ft. Casts light shade.
Betula Birch	Cheap and easy to find large specimens. Pretty leaves, white bark. Some have lovely weeping form.	Can take a couple of years for the bark to colour.	In 3yrs about 8ft. Casts light shade.
B. p. 'Youngii'	Compact weeping form.	Doesn't like heavy clay.	In 3yrs about 6ft. Casts heavy shade.
Catalpa bignonioides	Huge green leaves and delicate white flowers.	Late into leaf. Takes years to flower. Expensive.	In 3yrs about 6ft. Casts heavy shade.
C. 'Aurea'	Huge golden leaves.	Late into leaf. Needs some shelter. Expensive.	In 3yrs about 5ft. Casts heavy shade.
Cotoneaster 'Cornubia'	Good screening tree. Red berries until midwinter. Evergreen.	Can be burnt in strong cold winds. Boring in summer.	In 3yrs about 8ft. Casts heavy shade.
Crataegus Hawthorn	Very tough. White, pink or red flowers and coloured fruit. Attractive to wildlife.	Slightly dull in summer.	In 3yrs about 8ft. Casts medium shade.
Eucalyptus gunnii	Wonderful grey aromatic foliage. Smooth bark. Evergreen.	Can be blown over in strong winds.	In 3yrs about 12ft. Casts light shade.
Gleditsia triacanthos 'Sunburst'	Stunning gold foliage. Very tough, attractive in wind, interesting form.	Very late to come into leaf.	In 3yrs about 7ft. Casts light shade.

Trees

Name	Good Points	Disadvantages	Vital Statistics
Laburnum watereri 'Vossii'	Lovely strings of yellow flowers in late spring. Nice weeping shape.	Unsightly seed heads. Poisonous seeds. Ugly in winter.	In 3yrs about 7ft. Casts medium shade.
Malus floribunda Flowering Crab Apple	Very prolific flowerer. Pink buds and carmine flowers. Nice weeping form.	Slow to establish.	In 3yrs about 7ft. Casts medium shade.
M. hupehensis 'John Downie'	White flowers. Golden fruit flushed with crimson.	Quite dull in spring and summer.	In 3yrs about 7ft. Casts medium shade.
Prunus Cherry	Flowers of all colours; some trees have lovely bark, some have good weeping form.	Most are ugly in winter. They don't grow old gracefully.	In 3yrs about 7ft. Casts medium shade.
P. 'Amanogowa'	Amazing column shape. Pretty pink flowers in spring.	Dull in summer and winter. Coarse leaves.	In 3yrs about 7ft. Does not cast shade.
P. subhirtella 'Autumnalis Rosea'	Attractive flower from Nov– March. Great autumn colours.		In 3yrs about 6ft. Casts light shade.
Pyrus salicifolia 'Pendula' Weeping Pear	Attractive grey-downy leaves with lovely weeping shape.	Slow to establish. Grows very wide.	In 3yrs about 6ft. Casts heavy shade.
Rhus Sumach	Attractive umbrella shaped tree. Stunning autumn colours – deep, fiery red.	Late to come into leaf. Spreads wide. Very odd in winter. Mostly only small specimens available.	In 3yrs about 5ft. Casts medium- to heavy-shade.
Robinia pseudo-acacia 'Frisia'	Fabulous golden foliage which moves nicely in the breeze.	Breaks easily so needs good staking. Very late into leaf.	In 3yrs about 8ft. Casts light shade.
Salix sepulchralis 'Chrysocoma' Weeping Willow	Good for summer screening. Gracious weeping form. Good for a moist position, wonderful near water.	Grows huge. Dries out a large area around it. Dangerous for foundations of walls and buildings.	Very fast-growing. In 3yrs about 10ft. Casts heavy shade.
S. caprea pendula	Incredibly narrow weeper. Stunning catkins in early spring.	Looks unnatural.	Slow-growing. In 3yrs about 6ft. Casts heavy shade.
Sorbus aucuparia Mountain Ash	Bright orange/red berries. Great autumn colours. Cheap.	Dull in summer.	In 3yrs about 8ft. Casts medium shade.
S. vilmorinii	Attractive fine foliage. Rose red berries which turn pink.	Can be difficult to obtain.	In 3yrs about 7ft. Casts medium shade.
Syringa Lilac	Lovely scented flowers in June. Lots of colours available.	Short period of interest. A bit invasive.	In 3yrs about 6ft. Casts medium- to heavy-shade.

Hedges (evergreen unless stated otherwise)

Name	Good Points	Disadvantages	Vital Statistics
Aucuba Laurel	Tolerates deepest shade. Interesting choice of leaves and berries when male and female present.	Can grow very wide. Difficult to cut. Looks a bit gloomy.	Slow-growing. Expensive.
Berberis	Delicate flowers in May, some with berries to follow. Natural shape. Thorny, so good protection.	Unruly growth and can get wide. Quite difficult to cut. Some not very dense.	Medium-growing. Medium-priced.
Buxus Box	Good-looking, compact, tough. Very easy to maintain.	Used more for creating ornamental edges than for privacy.	Very slow-growing. Small: cheap. Large: expensive.
Carpinus Hornbeam	Beautiful, natural hedge. Attractive leaves which go brown and stay on through winter. Stays narrow.	Usually only available as open-ground plants so plant in autumn or early spring. Slow to get established.	Slow- to medium-growing. Cheap.
Crataegus Hawthorn	Pretty flowers in spring if unclipped. Natural hedge, good for wildlife and good protection.	Plant in autumn or early spring (see above.) Grows quite wide. Tough to cut.	Slow- to medium-growing. Cheap. Deciduous.
Cupressocyparis leylandii	Unbelievably quick. Available everywhere and in most sizes. *C.l.* 'Gold Rider' (gold form) looks interesting.	Dull. Needs lots of clipping. Very greedy.	Very fast-growing. Medium-priced.
Escallonia	Attractive dark glossy foliage and range of pretty flowers. Good near the sea.	Doesn't like cold, wet winters. Grows wide. Not very hardy.	Medium-growing. Medium-priced.
Fagus Beech	Attractive leaves. Good autumn colours. Leaves go brown and stay on through winter. Narrow grower. Good for wildlife.	Plant in autumn or early spring. Slow to establish. Difficult to cut.	Slow- to medium-growing. Medium-priced.
Lavandula Lavender	Lovely low hedge. Grey evergreen leaves; blue or white flower all summer. Scented. Good for a cottage garden.	Likes good drainage. Dislikes cold, wet winters. Can get leggy. Pink is a bit disappointing.	Very slow-growing. Cheap.
Ligustrum Privet	Green or variegated leaves. Very dense and easy to clip. Good background and for formal effect.	Very greedy. Slow to get established. Can get diseased, usually in autumn.	Slow-growing. Cheap.

Hedges

Name	Good Points	Disadvantages	Vital Statistics
Lonicera nitida	Green or gold leaves. Gold is stunning. Very tough.	Can be difficult to keep narrow.	Medium-growing. Medium-priced.
Prunus lusitanica Portugal Laurel	A large glossy leaf. Tough and heavy. Very dense.	Very greedy – can get huge. Doesn't like to be kept too small. Grows wide.	Medium- fast-growing. Medium-priced.
Pyracantha	Pretty white flowers. Nice berries if left unpruned. Thorny, so good protection.	Difficult to clip. When clipped loses the berries. Gets burnt in wind.	Medium-growing. Medium-priced.
Ribes sanguineum Flowering Currant	Nice pink flowers in spring with unusual scent. Natural looking.	Grows large and wide. Flowers for a short time. Foliage is dull.	Medium-growing. Medium priced-cheap. Deciduous.
Rosa Roses	Various lovely scents and colours. Some of the old-fashioned ones are particularly good.	Gets many pests and diseases. Difficult to clip. Rose replant disease makes it difficult to replace a single damaged bush in a hedge.	Medium-growing. Medium-priced. Deciduous.
Rosmarinus officinalis Rosemary	Lovely aromatic leaves. Pretty pale blue flowers. Dark compact foliage. Delicious herb.	Needs good drainage. Not reliably hardy.	Slow-growing. Medium-priced.
Santolina	Good near the sea. Attractive, aromatic, grey feathery foliage. Nice yellow flowers.	Not very hardy. Needs particularly good drainage.	Slow-growing. Medium-priced.
Tamarix	Great windbreak – good near sea. Attractive fern-like foliage and pink or red flowers.	Ugly when pruned back.	Medium-growing. Medium-priced. Deciduous.
Taxus Yew	Wonderful thick foliage. Forms a very dense barrier. Good foil for other plants.	Berries are poisonous.	Extremely slow-growing. Expensive.
Thuja	Nice aromatic foliage. Good range of shades of green. Easy to clip and keep formal.	Dull most of the year. Small plants are unimpressive.	Fairly fast-growing. Medium-priced.
Viburnum tinus	Evergreen with flowers all through winter.	Slow to establish. Grows wide. Looks gloomy in summer. Doesn't enjoy tight clipping.	Fairly slow-growing. Medium-priced.

Large shrubs

Name	Good Points	Disadvantages	Vital Statistics
Acer Japanese Maple	Huge variety of shapes and sizes. Very delicate foliage.	Dislikes wind and hot sun.	Likes semi-shade. Deciduous. Slow-growing. Very expensive.
Arbutus Strawberry Tree	Orange-red fruit in autumn at the same time as white flowers. Very dense foliage. Slightly peeling bark.	Prefers acid soil. Doesn't like cold wind or cold, wet winters.	Likes semi-shade. Evergreen. Slow-growing. Expensive.
Arundinaria murielae Bamboo	Pretty leaves on yellow stems up to 7ft tall. Consider getting a big specimen.	Invasive when established. Prefers moisture.	Likes sun or shade. Evergreen. Medium-growing. Medium to expensive.
A. nitida	Interesting purple stems when young. Consider getting a big specimen. Sounds good in wind.	Prefers moisture. Invasive when established.	As above.
Aucuba Laurel	Most have variegated leaves. Scarlet berries if both male and female are present.	Not exciting at any time of year.	Likes shade- or semi-shade. Evergreen. Medium-growing. Medium-priced.
Berberis (Evergreen)	Many types, some with attractive orange flowers followed by berries.	Dull most of the year.	Tolerates most conditions. Evergreen. Growth varies. Cheap.
Berberis (Deciduous)	Many foliage colours from pure gold (*B. thunbergii* 'Aurea') to speckled purple (*B. thunbergii* 'Harlequin'). Great for late spring, summer and autumn.	Comes into leaf late in spring. *B. t.* 'Aurea' scorches in full sun.	Tolerates most conditions. Deciduous. Slow-growing. Cheap.
Buddleia Butterfly Bush	Lovely, scented flowers. Attracts butterflies. Many colours available. Very tough.	Can bully and overwhelm other plants. Not attractive in winter and early spring.	Likes sun or shade. Deciduous. Fast-growing. Cheap.
Camellia	Glossy dark green leaves and spectacular flowers in spring (colours from white to dark red with everything in between).	Dislikes morning sun. Loves acid soils.	Likes shade or semi shade. Evergreen. Slow to medium-growing. Expensive.

Large shrubs

Name	Good Points	Disadvantages	Vital Statistics
Choisya ternata Mexican Orange Blossom	Aromatic leaves and scented white flowers in May. Attractive light green leaves.	Can get leggy, particularly in the shade. Likes to be clipped after flowering.	Likes sun, tolerates some shade. Evergreen. Fairly fast-growing. Medium-priced.
Cornus Dogwood	Shrubby forms with coloured stems (red or yellow). Gold/green leaves are particularly good.	Hates to dry out. Once established, can become very wide.	Shade or sun. Deciduous. Medium-growing. Cheap.
Cortaderia Pampas Grass	Long strappy grasslike foliage and glorious plumes of flower. Good semi-screener. Sounds nice in wind.	Can take a long time to flower. Looks messy in winter.	Prefers sun. Deciduous. Fast-growing. Cheap.
Corylus avellana 'Contorta'	Unusual twisted stems. Looks bizarre in winter. Slender catkins in spring.	Somewhat grotesque in summer as the leaves look a bit curled up.	Shade or sun. Deciduous. Slow-growing. Medium-priced.
Cotinus coggygria Smoke Tree	Many have stunning purple leaves with good autumn colours. The flowers are quite delicate.	Late into leaf in spring. Spreads wide – cut back to strong buds in spring.	Likes sun. Deciduous. Medium-growing. Medium-priced to expensive.
Cotoneaster (Evergreen)	Leathery, glossy leaves. Very tough with red or yellow berries in autumn. Large range of shapes.	Dull for most of the year. Casts heavy shade.	Likes sun or shade. Evergreen. Growth varies. Cheap.
Cotoneaster (Deciduous)	Leaves grow in an attractive herringbone shape. Great autumn colours.	Slow growing. Never very spectacular.	Likes sun or shade. Deciduous. Slow-growing. Cheap.
Deutzia	Lovely pink or white flowers in spring.	Short period of interest. Messy and dull for much of the year.	Prefers sun. Deciduous. Medium- to fast-growing. Cheap.
Elaeagnus	Foliage from deep green to sharply variegated. Can be very bright – good for exposed position.	Very rigid form which looks a bit stiff.	Likes sun or shade. Evergreen. Medium-growing. Medium-priced.
Escallonia	Pink, white or red flowers. Glossy leaves.	Short period of interest.	Prefers sun. Evergreen. Medium-growing. Cheap.
E. 'Iveyi'	Scented.	Needs a sheltered site.	As above.

Large shrubs

Name	Good Points	Disadvantages	Vital Statistics
Fatsia japonica	Bold form with huge leaves. Very eye-catching. Weird white flowers. Good as a contrast plant.	Can be damaged in exposed positions.	Likes sun or shade. Evergreen. Medium to fast. Medium-priced.
Forsythia	Vivid yellow flowers in spring.	Ugly when not in flower, which is most of the time.	Likes sun or shade. Deciduous. Fast. Cheap.
F. suspensa	Softer yellow flowers.	As above.	As above.
Hamamelis Witch Hazel	Wonderful: scented flowers in winter (yellow or orange). Good autumn colours.	Doesn't like wind. Grows very wide. Not interesting in summer.	Prefers shade. Deciduous. Slow-growing. Very expensive.
Hibiscus	Brilliant, bright flowers in late summer. Vivid colours.	Very late into leaf, short season of interest. Prefers sheltered site.	Likes sun. Deciduous. Medium-growing. Medium-priced to expensive.
Hydrangea	A variety of very attractive flowers. Long flowering season. Some with great leaves (*H. villosa & H. sargentiana*)	Some of the flowers look very artificial. Can get quite wide.	Prefers shade. Deciduous. Medium-growing. Medium-priced.
Ilex Holly	Great variety of interesting foliage. Berries on female when there is a male nearby.	Very spiky foliage. Difficult to grow things under a holly.	Likes sun or shade. Evergreen. Slow-growing. Medium-priced.
Kerria japonica	Yellow pom-pom flowers in spring and summer. Pale green stems.	Can get invasive and messy.	Likes sun or shade. Deciduous. Medium-growing. Cheap.
K. j. 'Variegata'	Excellent, compact plant.	Slow-growing.	As above.
Kolkwitzia amabilis Beauty Bush	Graceful arching branches. Young foliage tinged pink. Pink flowers in June.	Gets big and very wide.	Likes sun or shade. Deciduous. Fast-growing. Cheap.
Laurus nobilis Bay Tree	Very dense. Aromatic leaves used in cooking. Pretty white flowers in summer.	Needs a sheltered site. Will not stand a cold, wet winter.	Likes sun. Evergreen. Slow-growing. Expensive.
Lavatera Mallow	Superb with pink, pale purple or white flowers which last for 6 months. Great value.	Can be shortlived (5–7 years). Best to cut back in spring.	Likes sun or shade. Deciduous. Fast-growing. Cheap.

Large shrubs

Name	Good Points	Disadvantages	Vital Statistics
Magnolia (Deciduous)	White, purple or pink tulip-shaped flowers in spring. Beautiful even when not in flower.	Short flowering period. Susceptible to late spring frosts.	Prefers semi-shade or sun. Fairly slow-growing. Medium-expensive.
Magnolia grandiflora (Evergreen)	Evergreen with huge glossy leaves and sensational scented flowers. Grows big.	Needs shelter. Buy one which flowers young or you might have to wait a long time.	Prefers sun. Medium-growing. Medium-expensive.
Mahonia	Very striking holly-like leaves, yellow scented flowers in winter. Very tough.	The dark foliage can look oppressive in summer.	Likes sun or shade. Evergreen. Medium-growing. Medium-priced.
Olearia Daisy Bush	Very good for a windy site. Stunning white flowers in summer.	Short period of interest.	Likes sun. Evergreen. Medium-growing. Medium-priced.
Osmanthus delavayi	Attractive green foliage, scented white flowers in May.	Short period of interest. Prefers the shelter of a wall.	Likes sun. Evergreen. Slow-growing. Medium-priced.
Philadelphus Mock Orange	Wonderful scented white flowers in May/June.	Can grow very big and leggy. Short period of interest. Messy.	Likes sun or shade. Deciduous. Fast-growing. Cheap.
P. coronarius 'Aureus'	Golden foliage.	Can burn in full sun.	As above.
P. 'Manteau d'Hermine'	Dwarf.	Short period of interest.	As above.
Phyllostachys aurea Bamboo	Lovely golden stemmed bamboo. Sounds good in wind.	Rather difficult to obtain. Specimens tend to be large and therefore expensive.	Likes sun or shade. Evergreen. Medium-growing. Expensive.
P. nigra Black Bamboo	Stunning black stems with small leaves. A wonderful plant.	Difficult to find and expensive.	As above.
Phormium New Zealand Flax	Very good looking spiky leaves in various colours from red to green and white.	Only hardy in a sheltered site. Needs protection in cold, wet winters.	Likes sun. Evergreen. Medium-growing. Expensive.
Pieris	Young foliage is brilliant red. Keeps its buds through winter with lily of the valley-like flowers in spring. Some have variegated leaves.	Prefers an acid soil and dislikes very dry soil or a hot position.	Prefers semi-shade. Evergreen. Medium-growing. Medium-priced to expensive.

Large shrubs

Name	Good Points	Disadvantages	Vital Statistics
Rhododendron	Loads of varieties, with a wide range of flowers and leaves. New ones being introduced all the time.	Loves acid soil. Many have a short flowering season.	Prefers sun. Evergreen. Medium-growing. Medium-priced.
R. 'Silver Edge' & *R.* 'President Roosevelt'	Attractive variegated leaves.	As above.	As above.
R. yakushimanum and related hybrids	Ideal for smaller gardens: compact, dark foliage, young leaves covered in grey down and stunning flowers.	As above.	As above, but medium-expensive.
Ribes sanguineum Flowering Currant	Masses of pink hanging flowers. The flowers (and leaves) have a curious scent.	Gets huge and has only a short period of interest.	Likes sun or shade. Deciduous. Fast-growing. Cheap.
Sambucus racemosa aurea Golden Cut-leafed Elder	Golden-cut foliage can be stunning, particularly in early summer.	Can get leggy. Late into leaf, early to drop leaves. The leaves burn easily in summer.	Prefers mixed sun and shade. Deciduous. Fairly fast-growing. Medium-priced.
Spiraea	Many different sizes and colours of flower.	Some have a short period of interest. They easily get scruffy and mildewy.	Likes sun or shade. Deciduous. Fairly fast-growing. Cheap.
S. japonica 'Goldflame'	Gold leaves which look wonderful in late spring.	They easily get scruffy and mildewy.	As above.
Tamarix	Graceful feathery foliage combined with pink feathery flowers. Lovely semi-screen.	Can get leggy and loose. Unattractive in winter.	Likes sun or shade. Deciduous. Fairly fast-growing. Cheap.
Viburnum	Huge variety of wonderful plants, with a range of seasonal interest.	Some have a short period of interest.	Likes sun or shade. Evergreen or deciduous. Fairly fast-growing. Medium.
V. tinus	Evergreen with flowers all through winter.	Dull green in summer.	As above.
V. bodnantense	Scented pale pink flowers on bare stems in winter.	Can look poor in dry weather.	As above.
Weigela	Great foliage colour and pretty flowers in May.	Golden-leafed form gets scabby. Short flowering season.	Likes sun or shade. Deciduous. Fast-growing. Cheap.

Climbers and Wall Shrubs

Name	Good Points	Disadvantages	Vital Statistics
Actinidia chinensis Chinese Gooseberry	Huge hairy leaves and powerful stems. If you have both male and female and they are well protected it can fruit.	Can overwhelm and strangle things as it climbs. Not reliably hardy.	Likes sun. Deciduous. Climbs by twining. Fast-growing. Medium-priced.
A. kolomikta	Interesting pink blotched leaves in late spring/early summer.	Can take a long time to get established. Leaves lose their colour quickly in summer.	Prefers sun. Deciduous. Climbs by twining. Slow-growing. Expensive.
Akebia quinata	Attractive leaves, with a pink tinge when they are young. Chocolate-coloured flowers in early spring.	Needs protection from cold winds. Not reliably evergreen.	Likes sun or shade. Evergreen. Climbs by twining. Fast-growing. Medium-priced.
Campsis	Gorgeous large trumpet flowers in late summer.	Very late to come into leaf. Not bushy at base. Not very hardy.	Likes sun. Deciduous. Climbs by twining. Medium-growing. Medium-priced.
Ceonothus Californian Lilac	Vivid blue flowers in May/June, with dark green foliage. Many different shades of blue available.	Prefers a sheltered site, well-drained soil. Can get bare at the base.	Likes sun. Evergreen. Medium-growing. Medium-priced. Wall shrub.
Clematis	Huge range of flowers, some at all seasons. Some evergreen species (which need the shelter of a wall).	Can get clematis wilt. Some get thin at the base.	Likes sun or shade. Deciduous or evergreen. Climbs in various ways. Medium- to fast-growing. Cheap to medium-priced.
Fremontodendron	Brilliant, large yellow flowers all summer (May–October). Very fast growing.	Though evergreen, it tends to be ragged in winter. Needs a protected position.	Likes sun. Evergreen. Fast-growing. Expensive. Wall shrub.
Garrya elliptica	Amazing silver catkins all winter set off against very dark foliage.	Prefers a sheltered site. Can look a bit gloomy in summer. Slow to establish.	Likes shade. Evergreen. Slow-growing. Expensive. Wall shrub.
Hedera Ivy	Many different leaf colours and shapes from pure gold (*H. helix* 'Buttercup') to dark green (*H. helix* 'Hibernica')	Can be slow to get started (especially *H.* 'Goldheart')	Likes sun or shade. Evergreen. Has aerial roots. Cheap- to medium-priced.

Climbers and Wall Shrubs

Name	Good Points	Disadvantages	Vital Statistics
Humulus lupulus aureus Golden Hop	Bright golden foliage, hop-fruit in autumn (scented of beer).	Difficult to buy an established specimen. When established, spreads fast and can overwhelm.	Prefers sun. Deciduous. Climbs by twining. Slow- to medium-growing. Cheap- to medium-priced.
Hydrangea petiolaris Climbing Hydrangea	Wonderful white lace-cap flowers in June. Interesting looking stems.	Slow to establish. Short flowering season.	Likes shade. Deciduous. Has aerial roots. Slow- to medium-growing. Medium-priced.
Jasminum nudiflorum Winter Jasmine	Yellow flowers in winter. Very tough, with an attractive, graceful form.	Takes a long time to get established, (then gets very big).	Likes shade. Deciduous. Needs tying. Medium-growing. Medium-priced.
J. officinale Summer Jasmine	Pretty, highly scented flowers in summer.	Can look untidy.	Likes sun. Deciduous. Medium-growing. Medium-priced.
J. stephanense	Pink flowers and slightly variegated leaves.	Can suffer in cold, wet winters.	As Summer Jasmine.
Lonicera Honeysuckle	Fabulous range of flower colours and scents. Some vigorous.	Some have a short season of interest. Can get bare at the base. Aphids love them.	Twining. Fast-growing. Shade or sun. Deciduous and evergreen. Cheap- to medium-priced.
L. japonica 'Halliana' and *L. j. repens*	Usually evergreen. Long flowering season.	Needs clipping in spring.	As above.
L. japonica 'Aureo-reticulata'	Gold speckled leaves.	Often gets mildew and can look poorly.	As above.
Parthenocissus Virginia Creeper and Boston Ivy	Great autumn colours and nice leaves in spring and summer.	Its aerial roots can damage old walls. Late into leaf.	Likes sun or shade. Deciduous. Aerial roots. Fast-growing. Cheap.
Pyracantha Firethorn	Loads of orange, red or yellow berries through autumn. Easy to grow.	Birds love the berries, particularly the red ones. Dull in summer.	Like shade. Evergreen. Medium-growing. Cheap. Wall shrub.
Polygonum baldschuanicum Russian Vine	Hugely vigorous – loads of flowers from summer to autumn.	Can become a terrible bully because of its vigour.	Likes sun or shade. Deciduous. Climbs by twining. Fast-growing. Cheap.

Climbers and Wall Shrubs

Name	Good Points	Disadvantages	Vital Statistics
Rhamnus alaternus 'Argenteo-variegata'	Interesting green and white foliage and nice tightly packed form.	Prefers a sheltered site.	Likes sun. Evergreen. Medium-growing. Medium-priced. Wall shrub.
Trachelospermum jasminoides	Nice glossy leaves with white flowers from summer to early autumn. Beautifully scented.	Likes a wall to protect it from the wind. Takes time to get established.	Likes sun. Evergreen. Climbs by twining. Medium-growing. Expensive.
Vitis Vine	Lovely autumn colours and delicious fruit.	Late to come into leaf. Needs careful pruning and sun to fruit.	Likes sun. Deciduous. Climbs by twining. Medium-growing. Medium-priced.
V. 'Brant'	Fruits easily although the grapes are not that good.	Can get mildew easily.	As above.
V. coignetiae	Huge stunning leaves but no fruit. Wonderful autumn colours.	Late to come into leaf.	As above but expensive.
Wisteria	Glorious bunches of blue or white flowers in late spring. Attractive leaves and stems. Beautiful even in winter.	Likes good drainage. See also 'Buying Plants'.	Likes sun. Deciduous. Climbs by twining. Fast-growing. Expensive.

CHAPTER NINE

Decorative Plants

There is one way of making a colourful garden: just use lots of colourful, decorative plants. That's fine if you want something that's bright and cheerful and don't mind if it is rather chaotic.

But, if you want something that looks more integrated and mature, you'll have to use a bit more cunning.

The problem

If you concentrate only on colourful flowering plants, your garden will probably look good for a short time but after everything has finished flowering, you'll be left with very little that's interesting.

What's frustrating is that you can't solve this problem simply by throwing more colour at the garden. You may have experienced this yourself: you plant a few bright things here and there, stand back to admire the effect and – where are they? Disappeared, merged into the general background.

Also, plants don't automatically work well together. French marigolds (bright oranges) and old fashioned roses (lovely subtle colours) look great separately but, when planted side by side, look wrong. The brightness of the marigolds makes the roses look wishy-washy and the informality of the roses makes the marigolds look artificial.

Finally, if all you do is use decorative plants like this, it will take a long time for the garden to look mature.

What follows aren't rules, they are just Instant Gardening suggestions.

Plant associations

A plant association is the way plants work together. On its own, a daffodil looks bright and jolly. Seen in a garden underneath, say, a magnolia in full bloom, it looks insignificant. Seen amongst snowdrops it looks bold, almost robust.

A good plant association is where two plants highlight each other's strengths. Whole books have been written about this, but the simplest way to think about it is to divide plants into ones that make their effect by one strong and vivid quality and those that make their effect in a less extreme way. For instance, dahlias make their effect because of their incredible colour. Roses appeal in a more subtle way.

The easiest way to make good associations is to ensure that bold plants stand out from their surroundings and that things that work in more subtle ways complement each other.

So it wouldn't be a good association to combine pastel-coloured plants and something similar but startling.

Imagine you have a space between a clump of light blue delphiniums and a pale pink spirea. A plant with extreme reds like the *dahlia* 'Bishop of Llandaff' with its beetroot coloured leaves and red flowers wouldn't flatter them. In fact, it would make the delphiniums and spirea look insipid. A much better association would be one that complemented the light colours. You might try something like a *Fuchsia magellanica* 'Versicolor' which has interesting pink and white leaves and little red flowers.

On the other hand, the dahlia 'Bishop of Llandaff' would associate well with a bush eucalyptus and a senecio, both of which have grey foliage. The splash of red against the dramatic grey would be fabulous.

These are not hard and fast rules – but they are useful to be going on with.

Successful beds

A bed is not just a block of plants surrounded by path and lawn. It should be a *group* of plant associations that make a single unit.

Beds in big gardens are fairly easy. You make sure the associations are successful by grouping plants by species ('the rose bed'), by season ('the winter garden'), by colour or by form ('the herbaceous border'). But in small gardens we don't have the space for these single theme beds. We have to make mixed beds, and getting the associations to work in them is more of a challenge.

Decorative plants and the framework

The first thing is to establish an overall shape. Use decorative plants to link together the framework.

Imagine that at one end of a bed an old wisteria climbs a wall. Several feet away a framework plant spreads across a manhole cover. You've used, say, a beautiful juniper (*Juniperus squamata* 'Blue Star' – a blue-grey evergreen which grows horizontally). What should go between them?

In one sense it could be anything you have to spare – bedding plants, herbs, whatever. But to look really good and instantly mature, it would be better to link the two framework plants. The wisteria climbs up the wall: the juniper spreads across the ground. If the plant between visually bridges the gap, all three will form a unit that will look excellent.

So you need something quite tall. If the spot is sunny, one of the big cistuses would be wonderful (an evergreen with pink flowers through summer and lovely aromatic leaves). If it is shady, a hydrangea might work (a summer flowering shrub with huge vivid pom-pom flowers).

Colour

The simplest, most Instant way to get a bed looking good is to limit the number of colours in it to three (these might be pink, grey and white). You could use any of the shades of these and any combination that the plant world provides: grey leaves; pink bark; white berries. Somehow, it makes the bed look like a single, natural group.

You shouldn't be religious about this. Some blues and yellows in amongst the greys and whites will add extra zest.

People worry too much about plants clashing. This shouldn't concern you except where you are sure plants are going to flower at exactly the same time. So a wisteria (light blue) doesn't clash with a *Hypericum patulum* 'Hidcote' (which is yellow) because the wisteria flowers in spring and the hypericum flowers in mid-summer. Far from clashing, they make a good association because their combined flowering season is so long.

Height

A bed with everything about waist height looks dull. One of the most Instant ways of making it look better is to introduce valleys, hills and peaks.

Try to make the transitions fairly smooth and natural; then interrupt them with the occasional, surprising exclamation mark. You could use *Prunus* 'Amanogawa' (a cherry that grows straight up); or *Juniperus chinensis* 'Skyrocket' (a slim blue-green conifer) or even a 'Ballerina' apple tree (which grows in a narrow column).

Seasonal interest

Now that plants are grown in containers, most people buy things when they look good, which is usually when they are flowering. So if you buy mostly in spring and early summer your garden will look good in spring and summer. Unfortunately it won't look all that impressive for the rest of the year.

So if possible, try not to buy all your plants at one time and in summer look ahead to winter and spring and buy plants that flower then.

Another solution is to get plants that don't depend just on flowering for their appeal.

Most plants only flower for a few weeks, months at most. By thinking about the other ways in which plants look good, your beds will look better for longer.

Fruit

This comes in all colours and sizes and shapes, usually in late summer or autumn. There are, for instance, vividly coloured rose hips, crab apples and berries.

Edible fruit are particularly good for small gardens since you get flowers in spring, beautiful looking fruit in summer and a tasty treat in autumn. Tree fruit on dwarf root stocks and 'Ballerina' apples are also ideal for small spaces.

Note: apples and pears need partners to produce fruit (they are not 'self-fertile'. Ask your plant retailer for suitable pairings or see booklist).

Foliage

Leaves can be fantastic: gold, grey, red, pink, silver, black, purple, and weird combinations of colours. This can give interest all year round. There are also foliage plants that put on a marvellous display in spring, autumn and winter.

Bark

This is mainly exciting in winter. There are all sorts of wonderful different barks: striped; speckled; peeling; polished. Bark comes in all colours – white, red, yellow, black.

Shape
Some plants have a distinct shape which creates a dramatic effect all year round. You can find spires, domes, columns, cushions, spikes, fans.

Vegetables
These can be very effective in a mixed bed. Cauliflowers and broccoli look startling; beans have great flowers and wonderful looking pods; the leaves of artichokes and lettuces add unexpected shape and colour.

Scent
Scent is a huge part of the appeal of a good garden. You can get plants that smell nice even in winter.

Aromatic foliage
This is lovely, especially in summer when the heat releases the scent from the leaves.

So imagine you have a small garden and want to put in a rhododendron. Instead of 'Scarlet Wonder', which, although gorgeous, is only interesting when it is in flower, why not go for one like *Rhododendron yakushimanum*. This has a superb, mounded form, very interesting leaves and lovely white flowers.

Clumping

Putting plants singly into a garden is like scattering 'Smarties' onto a patterned carpet. They just don't make an impact.

Instead of planting singly, try planting in groups of at least three. Use more than two because two of anything is a straight line and straight lines in gardens look unnatural. At once this will make the garden look mature, because one of the characteristics of a mature garden is that things have spread and multiplied. So a typical, newly planted garden has lilies flowering on their own. A mature garden has them in groups – as does an Instant Garden.

Small things need clumping in bigger groups than larger plants: snowdrops, for instance, should always be planted in tight groups of at least a dozen.

It is really a question of scale. If you have a fairly large garden and want a birch, it might be better to plant several together. The clustered white trunks look stunning, much better than just a single one.

This means, of course, that you should buy at least three of smaller specimens. At first it will seem odd not including every different variety you can. But planting in groups is a very cost effective way of adding colour to your garden.

Instant maturity

Another way of creating the effect of maturity is to ignore the planting advice on the label and to deliberately pack plants too closely together. This will make them look as though they have grown into each other (it also keeps weeds down).

Of course, after a couple of years you'll probably have to move something – but that isn't really a big price to pay for a lovely Instant effect.

Instant colour

On special occasions when you want the garden to look really good, use spot crops to give an extra zing. These are mostly bedding plants sold when they are flowering at their peak – polyanthus in spring, busy Lizzies in summer and pansies in autumn.

Restricting the number of different colours you buy is vital – too many different varieties will make the garden look a mess. Clumping is also essential – it will make the additions look more natural.

Some shrubs are spot crops and so serve both an immediate and a long-term purpose and can be more easily justified economically. These include hebes (flowers for 3 months in late summer), hardy fuchsias (some of which have beautiful foliage) and pots of flowering bulbs.

Slow-growing plants

To make the garden look okay while you wait for a marvellous but slow-growing plant to inch its way to maturity, you can use a cheap, fast-growing plant as a stop gap.

Imagine *Hedera helix* 'Goldheart' (a slow-growing ivy with a stunning, gold-splashed leaf) is creeping up a bare wall. The wall is, at the moment, an eyesore and likely to remain that way for years. Why not plant a fast-growing climber like Russian vine nearby? Russian vine is incredibly vigorous, with masses of small white flowers and will cover the wall quickly, dealing with the eyesore in the short term. Lead it away from the hedera which, over the years, will continue to grow. When the hedera is big enough, simply remove the vine.

Sun and shade

Beds in the sun should be treated slightly differently to those in the shade.

Bright flowers work well in the sun but shade seems to rob them of some of their appeal. In darker borders try light, pale flowers.

Lots of foliage plants prefer shade and this gives you the chance to create exciting schemes.

Remember that in a sunny bed you can use the ground under the larger plants for shade lovers.

Groundcover

Groundcover plants spread over the earth and are used mostly to suppress weeds. That makes them sound boring – and too often groundcover is just a dull carpet of green. It needn't be!

Try using some of the more exotic groundcover plants and put them in dense clumps in big groups. You'll discover that the effect is lovely. *Houttuynia cordata* 'Chameleon', for instance, has amazing rainbow-coloured leaves, as do some of the ajugas. *Euphorbia robbiae* is evergreen, tolerates the deepest shade and has weird green flowers with an interesting form. Even some of the periwinkles can look great: *Vinca major* 'Maculatum' has a gold splash on its leaves.

Winter interest

When planting things with winter interest, group them so that they make maximum impact and put them where they can be seen from the house (which is where most of us spend most of the winter). A mahonia (an evergreen shrub with a holly-like leaf and stunning yellow sprays of scented flowers in winter) at the back of a garden is a waste. A Christmas rose behind a rockery means you'll rarely see its startling white, winter blooms.

SUMMARY

To make the best Instant impact, when you do decorative planting consider:

- the conditions (these determine what will thrive)

- the size and shape needed to contribute to the bed as a whole

- when you want it to look good

- the plants around it and how it will associate with them

- whether you can create interest other than with flowers

- if you should use one specimen or a clump.

The charts that follow describe a few of the more commonly available plants. Many wonderful plants are not mentioned. However, thinking like this – in terms of advantages and disadvantages – is a great way of choosing any plant.

Larger decorative plants

Name	Good Points	Disadvantages	Vital Statistics
Azalea (Deciduous)	Lovely flowers in May with attractive autumn colours. Some are scented.	Need acid soil. Look a bit dull in summer and winter.	Likes sun or shade. Best in spring and autumn.
Azalea (Evergreen)	Tight glossy foliage with bright flowers in May.	Need acid soil. Fairly short period of flowering. Slow-growing.	Likes sun or shade. Best in spring.
Cistus	Attractive aromatic foliage. Colourful flowers, ranging from white to deep purple.	Prefers a sheltered site and well drained soil.	Likes sun. Best in summer.
Cytisus Broom	Lovely feathery form. Attractive for most of the year – feathery form and stunning flowers. Good in poor soil.	Can be short-lived. Worth cutting back after flowers have finished.	Likes sun. Best in spring.
Daphne odora 'Aureomarginata'	Evergreen with dark green leaves with gold margins. Fabulous scented purple flowers in February and March.	Not reliably hardy. Best in a sheltered site. Expensive and slow-growing.	Likes sun. Attractive all year round.
Fuchsia Hardy Fuchsia	A great range of flower and foliage colour. Very long flowering season. Cheap.	Late into leaf in spring.	Likes semi-shade or sun. Best in summer and early autumn.
Hebe	Glossy evergreen with many different flower colours. Long flowering season. Great value.	Larger leafed ones prefer a sheltered site.	Likes sun. Best in summer to late autumn.
Hypericum	Vivid yellow flowers. Most are evergreen.	Usually lose their leaves in cold areas.	Likes either sun or shade. Best in summer.
Lavandula Lavender	Pretty grey evergreen with lovely scented flowers all summer. Good value.	Likes good drainage. Can get leggy. Slow-growing.	Likes sun. Best in summer to early autumn.
Potentilla	Easy to grow, thrives in poor soil. Long flowering season and good range of colours.	Very late into leaf and gets untidy late in the year.	Likes sun. Best in summer to early autumn.
Senecio	Pretty furry grey leaves. Yellow flowers are bright and cheerful. Easy to grow.	Can get messy after 2–3 years so cut back in spring.	Prefers sun. Attractive all year round.
Skimmia	Attractive in bud all winter, pretty flowers in spring. Hermaphrodite form has berries. Otherwise need both male and female.	Needs an acid soil. Quite expensive. Never really spectacular. Slow-growing. Leaves often go yellow.	Likes shade. Best late autumn to early spring.

Smaller decorative plants

Name	Good Points	Disadvantages	Vital Statistics
Acanthus	Wonderful dark foliage. Remarkable flowers.	Takes time to get established.	Best period March–Sept. Likes sun.
Agapanthus	Stunning blue or white flowers.	Needs feeding to flower. Likes well-drained soil.	Best period July–Sept. Likes sun.
Alchemilla mollis	Pale green foam-like flowers. Pretty pale leaves.	Seeds itself all over the place.	Best period May–July. Likes sun or semi-shade.
Anemone hybrida	Attractive pink or white flowers late in summer.	Can get spindly. Buy well-rooted plants.	Best period Sept–Oct. Likes sun or semi-shade.
Aster novi-belgii Michaelmas Daisy	Stunning colours, flowers late in the year.	Some suffer badly from mildew.	Best period July–Oct. Likes sun.
Astilbe	Great value – attractive foliage and late, plume-shaped flowers.	Prefers moist position and mustn't get dry.	Best period July–Sept. Likes shade.
Bergenia	Huge floppy evergreen leaves. Red, pink or white flowers. Good weed suppressor.	Leaves can get blotchy after winter.	Year-round interest. Likes sun or shade.
Campanula	Huge variety of colour, sizes and shapes. Great in summer.	Can look scrappy after flowering.	Best period July–Sept. Likes sun or semi-shade.
Ceratostigma	Intense blue flowers very late in summer.	Hates cold, wet winters. Looks dull in spring.	Best period Sept–Oct. Likes sun.
Cheiranthus or *Erysimun* Perennial Wallflower	Attractive grey foliage with wonderful mauve flowers all season.	Hates cold, windy, wet winters. Can look scrappy in spring.	Year-round interest. Likes sun.
Crocosmia	Strap-like foliage with spikes of stunning red or orange flowers.	Because the colour is so intense, it can make nearby plants look dull.	Best period July–Aug. Likes sun.
Delphinium	Beautiful foliage and flowers ranging from white to dark blue.	Often needs staking. Give it plenty of space. Looks scrappy after flowering.	Best period June–July. Likes sun or semi-shade.
Dicentra Bleeding Heart	Lovely pink hanging flowers in May/June with attractive cut foliage. Nice white flowering form.	Looks shabby after flowering.	Best period May–Sept. Likes sun.

Smaller decorative plants

Name	Good Points	Disadvantages	Vital Statistics
Digitalis Foxglove	Looks natural – good for woodland and cottage garden.	Looks ugly after flowering.	Best period May–June. Likes sun or shade.
Euphorbia	Stunning foliage with a variety of weird flowers.	Can get a bit untidy after flowering.	Period of interest varies. Most prefer sun.
E. characias wulfenii	Evergreen with compact grey foliage.	Dislikes cold, wet winters.	Year-round interest. Likes sun.
Geranium	Fantastic range of colours. Very natural effect.	Looks untidy after flowering.	Best period May–July. Likes sun or semi-shade.
G. sanguineum lancastrense 'Splendens'	Low growing with a long period of flowering.	As above.	Best period. June–Oct. Likes sun or semi-shade.
Helleborus	Evergreen with stunning foliage and wonderful flowers in winter or early spring. Many interesting varieties.	*H. niger* can look untidy in summer.	Period of interest varies. Tolerates sun or shade. *H. niger* prefers shade.
Hemerocallis	Lovely lily-like flowers in various colours. New varieties have a longer flowering period.	Many have short flowering period. Untidy in leaf.	Best period in June. Likes sun.
Heuchera	Pale green leaves and pretty red/pink flowers.	A bit messy after flowering.	Best period July–Aug. Likes sun or semi-shade.
H. microantha 'Palace Purple'	Superb purple leaves.		As above but best period May–Oct.
Hosta	Stunning foliage with attractive flowers. Leaves often variegated.	Slugs love them.	Best period Aug–Oct. Likes shade.
H. sieboldiana	Huge grey/blue leaves.	As above.	As above.
Iris	Long-stemmed flowers and attractive spiky leaves.	Short flowering season.	Best period June–July. Likes sun or semi-shade.
I. unguicularis	Flowers in winter.	As above.	Best period Nov–March. Likes sun or semi-shade.
Lobelia cardinalis	Attractive red foliage and spikes of intense red flowers.	Can be difficult in cold wet winters.	Best period June–Oct. Likes sun or semi-shade.

Smaller decorative plants

Name	Good Points	Disadvantages	Vital Statistics
Lupinus Lupin	Stunning vivid flowers. Attractive leaves in spring.	Looks scrappy after flowering. Aphids love them.	Best period May–Aug. Likes sun or semi-shade.
Nepeta Catmint	Vivid blue flowers and nice grey foliage.	Can be difficult in cold wet winters.	Best period July–Sept. Likes sun.
Paeonia Peony	Huge flowers and attractive oriental-looking foliage.	Shy to flower when young. Very short flowering season. Hates being transplanted.	Best period in May. Likes sun or semi-shade.
Papaver Poppy	Very vivid flowers. Many different colours available.	Short season and messy after flowering.	Best period June–July. Likes sun.
Penstemon	Range of marvellous flowers in apricot, white and crimson.	Not entirely hardy.	Best period July–Oct. Likes sun.
Phlox	Many vivid colours – lovely cottage garden effect.	Prone to mildew, flowers need support and looks poor after flowering.	Best period July–Sept. Likes sun.
Scabiosa Scabious	Pretty pastel flowers throughout summer.	Can get scrappy.	Best period March–Oct. Likes sun or semi-shade.
Sedum (Autumn flowering)	Pale flowers late in summer. Thick, glossy leaves.	Dull in spring.	Best period Sept–Oct. Likes sun.
Tradescantia	Blue, purple, claret or white flowers with narrow foliage.	Messy habit of growth.	Best period Sept–Oct. Likes sun.
Verbascum	Spiky flowers in many different colours including apricot. Some have huge furry leaves.	Can be short-lived.	Best period July–Sept. Likes sun.

Groundcover

Name	Good Points	Disadvantages	Vital Statistics
Arundinaria pygmaea Groundcover Bamboo	Pretty, low-growing evergreen.	Slow to start, but very invasive once established.	Likes sun or shade. Expensive.
Cistus corbariensis	Evergreen with lovely flowers in summer.	Likes good drainage. Gets quite tall.	Likes sun. Medium.
Cornus canadensis	Weird white flowers followed by fruit. Good autumn colours.	Difficult to establish. Slow-growing.	Likes shade. Expensive.
Convolvolus cneorum	Grey evergreen foliage with trumpet-shaped white flowers.	Can look scrappy in early spring. Slow-growing.	Likes sun. Medium-priced.
Epimedium	Pale leaves turning bronze in winter. Delicate flowers in spring. Great under trees.	Slow to get established.	Likes sun or shade. Medium-priced.
Euonymus fortunei 'Emerald 'n' Gold' and 'Emerald Gaiety'	Evergreen: brightly variegated leaves.	Should be trimmed back in summer. Slow-growing.	Likes sun or shade. Medium-priced.
Euphorbia robbiae	Evergreen. Interesting lime-yellow flowers in early spring. Great in dense shade.	Dark green foliage can seem dull in summer.	Likes sun or shade. Medium-priced.
Fern	Wonderful range of leaves – some low growing. Excellent even for deep shade.	No flowers. Slow-growing.	Likes shade. Medium-priced.
Gaultheria procumbens	Dark foliage with red berries in autumn/winter.	Needs acid soil. Takes ages to get established.	Likes shade. Medium-priced.
Geranium	Lovely foliage and dainty flowers through summer.	Scrappy after flowering. Most die down in winter.	Likes sun or shade. Cheap.
Hedera Ivy	Many types. All tough, some with unusual leaves.	Very invasive once established.	Likes sun or shade. Medium-priced.
Hebe pinquifolia 'Pagei'	Silvery evergreen foliage with white flowers.	Dislikes cold, wet winters. A bit slow-growing.	Likes sun. Medium-priced.
Houttuynia cordata 'Chamelion'	Bizarre pink, green and red marbled leaves.	Can become a weed itself. Dislikes cold, wet winters.	Likes semi-sun. Medium-priced.
Pachysandra terminalis	Attractive pale green evergreen foliage.	The flowers are uninteresting.	Likes shade. Medium-priced.
Rosa Groundcover Rose	Newer varieties have a long flowering season and great colours.	Looks poor in winter and early spring.	Likes sun. Medium-priced.
Vinca Periwinkle	Evergreen: some variegated, blue, purple, or white flowers.	Very invasive. Can need cutting back in early spring.	Likes shade. Medium-priced.

CHAPTER TEN

Buying Plants

We've all been caught one way or another: by the cheap jeans that, after one wash, become not-so-cheap shorts; by the complicated computerised tools that aren't as accurate as the old-fashioned ones and are twice as difficult to use; by the exotic fruit tree that doesn't flower, let alone fruit, in this country.

Shopping is something you learn and you normally have to pay for the lessons. This Instant Gardening guide aims to save you that expense.

Some general tips

Most of us can't go out and re-stock the whole garden in one spending spree. So when you buy plants, concentrate your money on one area at a time. That means you will see Instant results after each shopping expedition.

Look for plants that are well-proportioned and bushy. In most cases, a good specimen is one with many stems coming from the base. When you put bushy specimens into the garden, they grow into robust plants.

Try to buy plants which are comparatively free of weeds, otherwise you're importing new weeds and weed seeds into your garden. Weeds also weaken a plant because they compete with it for resources, so your new plant will not be as vigorous as it should be.

Watering is a problem for plant retailers. If the soil has shrunk away from the sides of the pot, or the leaves are crinkled, it may be a sign that the watering has not been careful enough, which will have weakened the plant.

Avoid plants with yellowing leaves. These are usually a sign of mineral deficiencies.

If you can, test plant associations while you are shopping. Group the plants as they will be in your garden – but be kind to the retailer and put them back in their right place afterwards.

Increasingly, retailers buy plants from growers at the moment they look their best. So if you know what you want and there are only a couple of poor specimens in stock, find out when the retailer is ordering next and buy then.

Pot size
The plant should be the right size for the pot.

- Too small a pot
  If lots of roots are coming out of the bottom of the

pot, it means the plant is probably pot-bound. Other signs are: a plastic pot distorted by the pressure of roots; leaves which look starved, or simply a big specimen in a surprisingly small pot.

If the pot is much too small, the roots will have got very tangled and formed a dense block. Water can't reach the inside, which means these pot-bound plants are particularly vulnerable to drought.

• Too big a pot
If the plant looks small compared to the pot, it is probably over-potted.

Since plants are priced by pot size, over-potted plants are also over-priced.

Also, if the roots haven't filled the pot, earth falls away from them when you take the plant out, which can damage them.

Guarantees

Good plant retailers should give a guarantee, especially with expensive purchases.

Some Superstores already offer one, and the members of the Garden Centre Association are covered by an automatic one-year guarantee on all hardy plants. They display a blue GCA flag.

Miscellaneous

You can buy (and plant) most things all year round. But unless you have no choice, don't tempt fate by planting in a very cold or very hot spell.
One good reason for getting plants when they are in flower is that even colour photographs on labels aren't always accurate.

When you put a new purchase into the garden, remove the label and keep it. You'll need it if you claim on a guarantee, and it also means you can take the plant back if you discover that it has been mislabelled.

Buying framework plants

If you buy small, you will have to wait years to really enjoy the framework plant. For Instant effect, buy the most mature specimen you can afford. That way you'll have years of extra enjoyment.

Imagine you decide to get a magnolia. A small one will remain insignificant for a long time. When it finally flowers you probably won't be excited by it anymore – and you may even have moved house. If you spend more and buy a larger one, it will probably flower in the first year. That will be exciting and make the whole garden look more special and interesting.

Fast-growing plants are an exception. Here, the difference between a big specimen and a small one may only be a single year's growth – but the big specimen will still probably cost much more than the small one, because you are paying for all the extras a big plant needs. With a large clematis, for instance, you pay for a big pot, a significant amount of compost and a hefty frame, which adds considerably to the bill. With a smaller clematis you only pay for a small pot, a little compost and a light cane, so it's much cheaper. And, as it's fast growing, that small clematis will take only a couple of years to cover a large area.

So if the framework plant is of a fast-growing variety, it sometimes makes sense to get a smaller plant.

Mature size

While on the subject of size, check with the supplier about how big your new framework plant is going to become and how long it is going to take to get there (unless you are positive you are not going to live in that house for long). Many people are unpleasantly surprised when a small tree grows big and bullying within just a few years. Weeping willow, for instance, is often sold as a specimen 6ft high. Within five years it can be 20ft tall. And that's only a start.

Shape

When faced with a number of specimens of the same variety, it is tempting to go for the tallest one. This is a fine way of buying firewood, but not so smart for gardening.

With framework plants, pay attention to their shape. Check all the available stock and choose the one that will look best in your site, doing the job you want it to do.

Very large specimens

It's cheaper to buy large trees grown in the open ground rather than container-grown trees. These open ground trees should only be planted from autumn to early spring. The varieties grown in open ground tend to be those used by the local Council or big landscape contractors. They include birches, cherries, alders, limes and oaks. You have to take particular care with them, because transplanting is a big shock to their system.

Some really large plants are imported from hotter climates and are best planted out in summer when they won't suffer too much from a sudden change in temperature. They include magnolias, bamboos, wisterias, hardy palms, and hollies. If in doubt, ask.

More buying tips

Plant retailers

There are plenty of excellent retailers, people who know and love plants. Talk to them, ask their advice, develop a relationship. It will pay off very quickly.

Beware of buying from bad retailers. Whatever you buy from them will probably disappoint. Plants are living things and a few weeks of really shabby treatment discourages even the toughest.

Bedding plants

If you buy bedding plants early in the year, ask the retailer if they have been hardened off (this means that they have been acclimatised to the cold by the grower). If not, you risk losing them if it gets chilly. Bedding plants are particularly vulnerable to drying out. Check that the compost hasn't shrunk away from the side of the container.
Bedding plants are grown in several ways.

Strip bedding
Seedlings are grown in polysytrene trays and sold in strips. This is the cheapest way of buying – but when you plant them out the roots sometimes get damaged.

Double sixes
Seedlings are grown on in larger polystyrene cells. It's more expensive but much more Instant because the plants are big and strong. Usually available in late spring.

Cell bedding
Seedlings are grown in individual cells in a polystyrene tray. Slightly more expensive than strip bedding – but the plants don't suffer root damage when they are put into the garden.

Pot bedding
The plants are quite large and usually in flower. They are Instant but not cheap.

Climbers

It is difficult not to damage a climber if it is very tangled, so look for neat specimens.

Climbers that are loose in the pot are often damaged at the base. Check that the support (cane or frame) is secure in the pot.

Roses

The cheapest are root-wrapped roses which are simply taken out of the ground and put into plastic bags. These are becoming less easy to find and are often of variable quality. Buy in autumn.

When buying roses in leaf, check they are disease-free. The main things to avoid are smudgy white powder on the leaves (mildew) and circular black marks on the leaves (black spot).

A good plant is one which has a lot of stems coming out from low down or, if it's a standard, from the head.

Wisterias

A seedling wisteria will take up to 12 years to flower, so it is better to get one which is grafted or layered. Check with the retailer when you can expect it to flower. If you want to be absolutely sure, buy plants with flower buds in April and May.

Herbaceous plants

You used to have to buy and plant in spring but nowadays the best plants are grown on in containers and are available throughout summer in bud or even in flower. They can be planted out like this.

It sometimes makes sense to buy a big specimen, rather than several smaller ones, because with the big specimen you get an Instant clump. If it is very big, you can split it and get several small plants which, put in a group, will make a really impressive effect.

Out of season

Some plants are produced and sold flowering out of their normal season. You can, for instance, find delphiniums, which normally flower in summer, fully budded in September.

These plants will revert to their normal flowering period the next season after planting.

CHAPTER ELEVEN

Planting

Planting seems simple and Instant enough. You dig a hole and drop the plant into it.

But since planting is an essential part of Instant Gardening, it is worth taking some extra care. Giving plants star treatment only takes a moment longer and will make a great difference for years.

When you remove a specimen from its pot, you will often find the roots have grown around the inside of the container. If you don't untangle them, they will take a long time to move into the surrounding earth and the plant will suffer. Also, if the ball of roots is too compact, water won't penetrate it and the plant can easily dry out.

To prevent this, carefully tease out the roots, breaking as few as possible. Put the plant into a hole big enough for them in their free state.

This doesn't apply to magnolias and ceanothus which hate root disturbance.

Ideally the hole should be just deeper than the depth of the pot. Into the bottom of it put some compost and bone meal.

The compost can be either tree and shrub planting compost or peat or – for all but the acid-loving plants – mushroom compost. For acid-lovers use the ericaceous composts. Use a couple of shovelfuls for big specimens, a handful for a small bedding plant.

Bone meal is a long-term fertiliser that nourishes roots. It will give the plant a real boost for at least a year. Use two handfuls for a big tree, one for a shrub. Mix it into the soil because it burns roots when it is neat.

Fork the soil conditioner and the bone meal into the soil at the bottom of the hole. This is wonderful for your new plant. It's also a good idea to mix some conditioner and bone meal into the soil that is going back into the hole.

Put the plant into the hole, stand back and look at it. Rotate it till the most attractive side faces forward.

Return the excavated soil, firm it and water thoroughly (use a lot, at least a couple of big watering-cans for a large shrub). Keep moist, but not waterlogged, for several weeks. With a large plant, water it for longer. The most common reason that newly planted specimens die is that they aren't watered enough.

Note on peat
There are two kinds of peat: Irish moss and sedge.

- Irish moss is brown, very acid and relatively inexpensive. It must be thoroughly wetted before you use it because it is packed stone dry and, in this state, repels water. It is suitable for acid-loving (ericaceous) plants.

- Sedge peat (sometimes called 'rich dark peat' or 'Somerset peat') is black, quite acid and is packed slightly moist so doesn't need such careful wetting before use.

Staking

Shrubs and conifers that are bottom-heavy don't need staking. Trees and standards, that carry most of their weight at the top, do.

To minimise damage to the roots, put the stake in after placing the tree in the hole but before the earth goes back. If possible, put it behind the trunk, as seen from the main view. The stake should only extend about halfway up the trunk to allow the trunk to flex and grow strong.

If you haven't got a suitable stake in your garden, remember to buy one when you get the plant.

It doesn't make sense to tie the plant to the stake by a bit of eye-catching rope. A tree-tie is much better. These are broad plastic ties which you can loosen as the tree grows. They are unobtrusive, reliable and not expensive. Don't use wire, it cuts into the bark as the trunk thickens.

Bedding plants

If your soil is good, you can just pop the bedding plants into holes. They will be so relieved to be free and unconfined that they'll race ahead.

If the soil isn't so good, put a few handfuls of loam-based compost ('Universal compost' or John Innes Number 2) beneath each.

Bulbs

The general rule is to plant bulbs deep enough to be covered with twice their own depth of soil. However, if you plant them late in the year, make the hole shallower and they will come up on time.

In common with most plants, bulbs appreciate a little good stuff beneath them (some rich compost). Lilies should be put on sharp sand because they need excellent drainage.

Clematis

These like to have their roots shaded. If planted in a sunny position, use something like a tile or slate to protect their roots.

'Clematis wilt' attacks them occasionally. This is a disease which kills everything above ground – astonishingly quickly, in about four days. To protect your new plant, make the planting hole sufficiently deep for the lowest bud to be buried under soil. If the virus hits, cut everything back to ground level. When the new shoot appears, spray it with 'Benlate'.

Roses

New roses won't thrive where old roses used to grow. This is called 'rose replant disease'. No-one knows for certain what causes it.

If you've got no choice of position, replace the old soil with new soil for at least 2ft around the site of the old rose and to a depth of 2ft – which is an awful lot of work just for a rose.

When planting root-wrapped roses, don't simply drop them into a small hole. First spread the roots, which have been confined, and dig a hole that is big enough for them.

Vegetables

In the main they like good, rich soil. Dig in plenty of good compost, well-rotted manure and the like.

Herbs

Rosemary, thyme, bay and sage taste better when the soil is poor. Parsley, chives and mint do better in rich soil.

Grey-leafed plants

They tend to be greyer in soil that has not been enriched (lavender, senecio, artemesia, teucrium).

Vines and Figs

Both produce better fruit in poor, well-drained soil that has not been enriched.

The roots of a fig also need to be restricted. Plant with stones in the hole or by a wall on a patio (which restricts the amount of water it gets) or in a container sunk in the ground.

Aerial rooting climbers

Some climbers, like ivy and Virginia creeper, root into walls. To encourage them, angle one branch back and tie it to the wall.

Transplanting

Instant Gardeners don't hesitate to move their plants around. You clumped some small plants and they've grown huge – move them: a decorative shrub is now big enough to do a framework job – transplant it; something hidden at the back of a border looks great in winter – bring it to the front.

People used to believe that you could only transplant in autumn and early spring. But it is generally possible to transplant things at other times of year, especially if you stick to a few simple guidelines:

- The longer a plant has been in one place, the more difficult it will be to move. If you decide to have a go at a long-term resident, expect it to be heavy digging and water it a lot after it has moved.

- Don't move something when it is about to, or is, flowering.

- The more root you can save the better.

- It's asking too much to move things in hot, dry spells.

- Don't move plants in very cold spells.

- Bigger plants are *much* harder to transplant than smaller plants.

Moving big plants
Lifting small plants is quite easy because their roots fit onto a spade. Big plants are more of a problem.

- Dig your spade into the earth a couple of feet from the trunk. If you immediately encounter thick roots, you are too close. No resistance means you are too far from the trunk (too much earth on a rootball is as bad as too little: a big mass of earth unsupported by root will collapse, pulling roots with it.) You are the right distance from the trunk when you feel the spade cut through fine roots.

- Dig down a fair way before you begin to cut under the trunk. Once again, feel for roots.

- With anything bigger than a big shrub, you are bound to cut some major roots. Don't worry – if you water the plant well it should survive.

- If it's a big job, don't tackle it on your own.

- If you have dug up a big root ball, carry it from the old place to the new one in a 'Bosbag' or a barrow (so that the root ball is supported).

- Lighten the load on the roots by stripping off some leaves or even pruning it once in its new home. If it is a very valuable specimen, or a large evergreen, it might be better to wait till autumn or early spring. You could also use 'Spray 'n' Save', a spray which seals the surface of leaves, minimising water loss.

Some plants hate being moved: magnolias, ceanothus, peonies, alstroemarias. But, with care (and luck) it can be done.

Once something is replanted, water it constantly. If it is big or the weather is hot, put a dripping hose at its roots.

It's worth noting that even the best gardeners sometimes lose things when they transplant them. That's gardening: take no prisoners, give no quarter.

CHAPTER TWELVE

Pots and Tubs

In most gardens there are some plants in containers: perhaps a couple of pots of geraniums on the patio; urns with lobelia and alyssum by the front door, or window boxes of petunias and pansies.

This is lovely – but unnecessarily limited. Plant containers can be used in more exciting ways.

What about putting a big plant in a big pot boldly into the middle of a flower bed? It will look marvellous, particularly if the pot is attractive. The plant starts above the level of everything else which gives added interest and the pot acts as a foil for all the plants around it.

This is a fine way of cultivating an acid-loving plant where the soil is very alkaline, and also one of the best ways, in a small garden, of growing something invasive like a bamboo.

You can do the same with indoor plants in the summer. They will thank you for it, and species like palms and cacti associate surprisingly well with bedding plants, particularly the more gaudy ones.

Any level surface is a place for a pot or a window box. A line of window boxes looks great on the top of a brick wall; wide steps are suitable for herbs in pots; the ideal thing to put on a manhole cover is an ornamental pot plant.

Use clumping. Several pots together make more impact than the same number spread around.

Most of us put hanging baskets near the house. But they are also very effective seen from a distance. Stout tree branches are great supports for hanging baskets, as are brackets on fence posts. Experiment with them low down, which can look surprisingly good.

You can even put pots into a pond. This is a lovely way of growing moisture-loving plants like bamboos, houttuynias or cyperus grass (which loves to be outdoors during the summer. Only the bottom couple of inches should be submerged.)

What can you grow in pots?

Anything and everything. There are obvious physical problems but, if you really wanted to, you could grow a tree in a pot.

So, be bold and use something unexpected when, for instance, you plant a window box. Why restrict yourself to dwarf conifers and bedding plants? Try things like variegated hebes, *Pieris japonica* 'Purity' or *Pieris japonica* 'Variegata'. Although they may outgrow the box within a couple of years, by then you'll have had a lot of pleasure.

It doesn't usually matter if the container is a bit small. Some plants – like lavenders, geraniums and nasturtiums – flower more profusely if they are in a pot which is a bit restrictive. This is probably why small window boxes often look so fantastic.

But there is a price to pay for squeezing a lot into a pot. The bigger the plant in relation to the container, the more regular the feeding and watering has to be. If you don't water a big plant that is in a small pot for even a short time, the plant will be damaged because there is no reservoir of water.

So the time you can afford to spend looking after your pots is an important limit on how many you have and how small a container can be. If you can't give it attention every day, use a bigger container.

There is also an obvious aesthetic consideration: a huge plant looks unnatural in a tiny pot.

Matching plants to pots
Where once there were just pots, and that meant clay, you now have glazed pots, Moroccan pots, Chinese pots, tubs, barrels . . . How do you make the best combination between plant and pot?

One suggestion – and you cannot be dogmatic in areas like this – is to try and match the plant to the decoration on the pot. For instance, a pot decorated with chrysanthemum-shaped flowers would be perfect for anything with similar shaped blooms. So you could put a flowering hibiscus into it with great success. Similarly, if blue is one of the colours in the decoration, you could match this with a plant with blue flowers. Plumbago, with its intense blue flowers, looks marvellous in this sort of pot.

You can put anything in a terracotta pot and it will look good.

If in doubt, use the garden centre stock to test the association when you buy the container.

Planting up

Pots look better packed with plants. Even where you are growing a specimen, put bedding plants around it to add more interest. Trailing plants that grow over the side of the pot and break up its lines are especially attractive (verbena, felicia, brachycome, lobelia).

But don't put a number of vigorous permanent things in the same container. They will just fight and none will do particularly well. A *Clematis montana* and a Russian vine in the same container will strangle each other above and below ground.

135

Potting compost

Use your own soil as long as you are confident that it is full of nutrients, drains excellently and is free of weed and disease. This is why so many gardeners use commercial potting compost.

Loam-based composts come in a variety of mixes. The most appropriate for containers are the ones described as 'Universal' composts (see Note below).

For acid-loving plants use ericaceous compost. This is based on peat, so these must be watered often enough to prevent them drying out. Once dry, mere watering won't get the compost wet again – you have to submerge the pot in water and leave it there until the peat absorbs some water (this is something to watch with all peat-based composts).

As long as the soil is well-drained and you feed the plant regularly, the soil shouldn't wear out. It's a good idea, though, to scrape off the top inch or so every couple of years and replace it with fresh soil.

Note Many loam based composts are made according to the 'John Innes' formula.

Number 1 is for seedlings.
Number 2 is for young plants.
Number 3 is for mature plants.

John Innes Number 3 is the most appropriate for containers.

Drainage

It's very important that a pot has good drainage.

- It must have holes in the bottom. Many barrels don't come with holes and you will have to make them (three or four half-inch-diameter holes every square foot).

- Put broken pots (crocks) over the holes to prevent them getting bunged up with earth.

- The compost must drain well. If you use your own soil, adding horticultural gravel helps.

Frost damage

Cold air sinks and, on a frosty night, will freeze an
unprotected pot. Tender plants (such as bay trees,
camellias, phormiums) many suffer root damage.

One way of protecting them is to encourage trailing
evergreens, such as a small-leafed ivy, to grow around
and over the pot. The leaves form a curtain that traps
a layer of warmer air which insulates the pot.

You can also swathe the pot with material in winter.
Use hessian or sacking.

Watering

To protect the surface beneath the pot from water, put
a saucer under the container.

But you shouldn't let plants stand in saucers of water
for too long because roots need air and, when soil
gets waterlogged, the plant can drown. More than a
couple of days is pushing your luck. A surprising number
of plants die this way.

During winter, don't water too much. Although the
soil shouldn't dry out completely, if it gets very wet the
roots, and even the pot itself, will be at greater risk of
frost damage.

Watch out for wind. A plant in a container has a
limited supply of water and so is vulnerable to
dehydration. The most practical precaution is to use
bigger containers in windy positions so the reservoir
of water lasts longer. Of course this also makes it less
likely that the pots will be blown over.

Types of container

DIY Containers
An old sink, bucket or yoghurt pot is free

But
People will often notice the container before they
  see what's in it

Terracotta
They look great and don't clash with anything
There are many different styles and designs
For something so attractive, they are not expensive
They age well
They drain well
Plants seem to like growing in them

But
They are fragile and, if bumped, will crack
When you buy, check carefully for hairline fractures
The designs change rapidly and matching or
  replacing an existing one can be surprisingly difficult
Large terracotta pots can be heavy
The earth in them dries out quickly
You should always ensure that you get ones which
  are guaranteed frost-proof, otherwise they will
  begin to flake in the winter

Compressed peat
Cheap
Can be planted straight out into the garden and the
  plant in it won't suffer at all

But
They don't last very long
If you try to move them when they are wet, they
  fall apart
They aren't attractive

Plastic Pots and Containers
Light – so good for roof gardens
Cheap
Won't break in a frost
Strong
Easy to replant the specimen
You can always get another if you want to replace
  one or make a pair
They come in many colours
Modern ones can look similar to terracotta or stone
  – although the really good imitations aren't much
  cheaper than the real thing (but are much lighter)

But
They generally look a bit cheap
They show the dirt quickly
They provide little insulation against frost

Wooden Versailles Tubs
Can be beautiful

But
Costly

Most require a plastic 'inner' – a tub to hold the earth

The Versailles tub itself needs regular maintenance with wood preservative

Wooden Barrels
If they have been burnt on the inside, they will last at least 10 years

Good value – especially the bigger ones which are usually old barrels, cut in half. The smaller ones are often custom-made for gardens, so can be more expensive than big ones

They are good insulation against frost

Tough and can withstand bumping

Easy to match or replace an existing one

Heavy – therefore difficult to steal

Can be painted or varnished to suit your garden

But
If the inside is not burnt, it will rot

You'll probably have to make drainage holes in the bottom

Can be difficult to transport and move

It is best if the metal bands are rivetted to the wood otherwise, when the barrel gets dry and the wood shrinks, they can simply slip off

You can't protect the ground underneath with a saucer

Concrete
Cheap

You can paint them

They are not heavy – especially if they contain glass fibre reinforcement (such as the Esplana range, which are good for roof gardens)

But
The cheapest ones look exactly like lumps of concrete

They chip easily

No matching saucers

Exotic Pots (Chinese, Thai, Moroccan etc)
Good value for something so ornate

Incredible range of sizes and designs

The big sizes are particularly impressive

They are more solid and robust than terracotta

But
Check that they are guaranteed against frost

They chip quite easily

Some are heavy, which can cause problems with delivery and moving

Reconstituted Stone, Ground Marble, Cement
Some wonderful classical designs

Some beautiful colours

But
They are costly

They are fragile – which can be a problem when you are installing them

They can be very heavy, and so difficult to transport, move and position

No matching saucers

Hanging baskets

Hanging baskets are often exposed to quite extreme conditions. A hanging basket by a wall might well be in direct sun for much of the day and get baked. A basket under a pergola might, on the other hand, be in shade for most of the day.

So it is best to decide where a basket is to go and then plant it with appropriate shade or sun-lovers, rather than plant the basket first, then put it somewhere and hope for the best.

Since baskets are exposed to the wind, watering is crucial. Of course, it's also a bit of a practical problem. Several modern developments help.

- There is specific hanging basket compost which contains a lot of water-holding material. This means you don't have to water so frequently.

- A 'Hi-lo' helps. This fits between hanging basket and support. When you want to work on the basket, you pull it down to a comfortable height. When done, you simply return the basket to its normal position.

- Alternatively, you can use a 'Pump-Can', a simple pump with a long spout which reaches high baskets.

- You can sink a small pot into the soil, its rim flush to the surface. When you water the basket, fill up the pot. It acts as a reservoir and gets water into the body of the basket.

- There are also drip irrigation systems that connect to a tap and remain in place permanently. To water and feed the basket, you simply turn on the tap.

When planting a hanging basket, don't be too conservative about what you use. Try some unusual things like herbs or heathers.

Pack the basket full of plants. That way, they'll flower profusely and you will see little of the basket itself.

Care

Watering systems
Automatic watering systems make it much easier to grow things in window boxes and pots. There is a discrete system which consists of a water regulator and narrow gauge pipes with different fitments on the end which go into the pot or hanging basket.

Feeding
Because the roots are restricted to the container, most plants in pots need feeding.

But since you don't want them to grow too much, don't feed them too often with fertilisers high in nitrogen, which encourage growth. Use these occasionally in spring and in early summer. Then, just before budding and during flowering, feed with a fertiliser that promotes flowers. These contain potash and are usually marketed as tomato feeds. That way you get more flowers and less foliage.

The law
When you move house, the plants in the soil belong to the new owner unless you agree otherwise. But the plants in containers belong to you.

Holidays
If you go away and can't get anyone to water your containers, move them into a shady position. If it is summer, put them on saucers, with a little water in them.

Even when someone has promised to water them, these precautions are still worth taking. No-one loves your plants quite as you do.

CHAPTER THIRTEEN

As the Garden Grows

In spite of its being a pleasant activity, a remarkable number of people find gardening a burden. When they think about it, it's in terms of duty: the lawn *needs* cutting; the weeding must be done; the roses *have* to be sprayed.

The Instant Gardener doesn't think like this.

We have gone through the regular jobs that 'have' to be done and tried to look at them from another point of view.

Do you really need to weed?
What happens if you don't feed?
Can you leave the pests and diseases alone?
What is the use of dead-heading?

Weeding

Most of us weed occasionally. But many of us feel it is not real gardening – it's more like tidying up, open-air housework. Is this true?

There are several reasons for weeding.

- Weeds compete with your plants for resources like water, nutrients and light.

- Some weeds are physically aggressive and invasive: bindweed, for instance, can smother most things; ground elder will spread through beds and overrun more delicate plants. Weeding will protect your plants against them.

- If the weeds in your garden are allowed to seed, you will be faced with very many more weeds in years to come.

- If their roots are allowed to run free, they will twine with the roots of your plants and getting them out will require hours of tedious, fiddly work.

So weeding helps those plants you have taken so much trouble to cultivate and also reduces work in the future.

That said, for all but the most formal gardens, if you don't weed regularly you won't notice that much. If you don't weed for several years, the garden will begin to look ragged. After a couple more years, the weeds will have taken over.

Prevention

Preventing weeds is much less trouble than getting rid of them.

You can discourage them by planting densely and using lots of groundcover. In densely planted beds, weeds have no room to grow.

If you want to leave bare earth between plants (either for aesthetic reasons, or to give the plants room to grow), you can prevent weeds from germinating by blanketing the surface of the beds with a top-dressing free of weed seed.

Peat is not very effective because it gets washed into the soil quickly. Forest bark is much better: although not cheap, it lasts for years and really does the job.

There are different kinds of forest bark. Choose the kind you like the look of: chipped, which comes in largish lumps and is very long-lasting, or the finer shredded bark.

Bark also conserves moisture in the soil. But the soil must be moist when you first spread it, otherwise you lock in the dryness and a serious drought can develop.

There are long-lasting chemical weedkillers which prevent weeds from germinating. These products are ecologically very suspect and we cannot recommend them.

Getting rid of weeds

Try to get them before they flower and seed. When you dig them up, remove as much root as you can, because lots of weeds can regenerate from a small section – bindweed, dandelion, ground elder and others.

Chemical weedkillers should only be used if you cannot weed any other way. Spray locally and mix small quantities so that little has to be thrown away. Some formulations use natural products and these may be preferable (for example, 'Amcide').

Weedkillers

Contact weedkillers are quick acting and kill anything green that they touch. These should only be used if weeding by hand is a problem.

Systemic weedkillers are taken into plants and go down to the root. They are often de-activated by contact with the soil. Use against weeds which propagate by root (brambles, bindweed, ground elder).

There are a few weedkillers that have a long-term effect on the soil (for example, sodium chlorate and SBK). These are very unpleasant chemicals and should only be used as a last resort for killing a stubborn tree stump or controlling brambles.

If you have children, buy weedkillers (and pest control chemicals) in child-proof packaging.

Paths

For most people it is enough just to run a spade along the joins in the paths cutting the weeds at the surface.

But if the weeds really bother you, use a long-term weedkiller like 'Pathclear'. Apply sparingly in the spring.

There are mixtures of detergent and algicide like 'Patio Jack' which help keep both terraces and paths clean and free of algae. Again, be careful how you use these chemicals.

Feeding

If you don't feed the garden, it won't suffer. Plants will continue to grow, flower and fruit.

But if you do feed your garden, it makes a surprising difference. Flowers will be bigger and brighter; fruit will be heavier; things will grow stronger and faster.

There are hundreds of plant foods. Some stimulate growth; others increase flowering; others promote root growth. To get the best results, don't overwhelm the garden; give the right one at the right time.

- Growth food should be used when growing is the main priority – for most plants that is spring and summer. Growth foods contain a lot of nitrogen – and say so on the packet. They are marketed as 'growth promoting' or as 'making leaves'.

- Food that stimulates flowering should be used mainly in summer. They contain plenty of potassium and are usually marketed as tomato food, or described as 'promoting flowering' or 'stimulates budding'.

- Root growth food should be given in autumn. Root growth foods are high in phosphates and include both autumn lawn feeds and bone meal.

- Some all-round foods are best given in spring (for instance, 'National Growmore').

Liquid feeds are taken up quickly – use in spring and summer for swift results. Solid feed is taken up more slowly and lasts longer – use in early spring and autumn.

Some fertilisers are absorbed by the roots, and some are foliar. These foliar feeds are absorbed directly by the leaves, which means they act quickly. They are generally used in summer when the leaf is very active and you want quick results.

The lawn

A traditional lawn puts a huge strain on soil. It grows in the same place year after year, and the soil never rests or gets replenished. If you don't feed, the grass will grow – but it won't be strong.

For a healthy, tough lawn, use plenty of fertiliser: for a mixed, meadow-like lawn, don't feed at all.

Spring

The specific spring fertilisers for lawns usually come as powders and often kill weeds and moss too.

Summer

During the growing season, give the lawn a regular dose of a high nitrogen liquid feed. The grass will grow greener, thicker and stronger.

Autumn

There are a number of granular feeds which are specifically for feeding the lawn in autumn. They help root growth and some have additives which kill moss.

Pests and diseases

In the past, people sprayed to prevent pests and diseases. We now know that this strips the garden both of the harmful insects and the beneficial ones. By spraying too enthusiastically, you are actually making things more vulnerable to attack.

So try to tolerate a few bugs and creepy crawlies. So what if a few plants get a little scabby? You'll find that once a natural balance is reached, nothing serious happens.

But occasionally that balance is upset and the pests race ahead. That's the time to intervene.

Most chemical companies are becoming ecologically aware and are putting safer chemicals on the market. They are promoted this way on the pack and you can encourage the trend by buying them. But it's worth noting that marketing men have gone ecology mad: everything seems to be ozone friendly now.

'Contact' insecticides kill what they touch. 'Systemic' insecticides are taken into the plant and kill the insects when they feed on it.

There are so many preparations on the market and new ones are being developed all the time that it would be pointless to detail exactly what to use against which pests. Instead this Instant guide makes general points.

Fruit and vegetables

If you want good-looking, unblemished produce you will have to intervene before pests strike. There are lots of books that go into the details (see booklist).

Blackfly and greenfly

Both contact and systemic insecticides work against these, but the sprays don't always get the young, so check for reinfestations.

White fly

Contact insecticides are not always effective. Use a systemic insecticide.

Scale insects

If the plant is small, you can remove them by hand (use a cotton bud, perhaps dipped in methylated spirits).

Otherwise use a systemic insecticide.

Slugs and snails

They can cause surprising damage.

In ecological terms, the safest way of dealing with them is to surround valuable plants with sharp sand or something similarly gritty (even forest bark helps). This works quite well but you have to renew the grit when earth mixes with it and it loses its sharpness.

You could also try setting traps. Sink saucers of beer into the bed so that the rim is flush with the surface. Although ecologically safe, they aren't that effective.

Against a bad infestation, try 'Fertosan'. This is relatively safe ecologically.

Traditional slug pellets are ecologically less safe but work well.

In the past few years, slugs have been rampant, and nothing, chemical or otherwise, seems to have dealt with them successfully. One technique which does hold them at bay is to go out at night with a torch and hunt them. They glisten in the dark. It's not exactly a safari, but it is an outlet for your feelings when your brassicas have been munched.

Mildew, blackspot and rust

These are worst on roses. They can all be treated by one chemical ('Systhane'). Some varieties are more resistant to these diseases, and if the problem is bad in your garden, it may be worth planting them.

With blackspot, get rid of all infected, fallen leaves in autumn as it will overwinter on them.

Hollyhocks and hypericum are susceptible to rust, and the plants may need to be destroyed if the treatments don't succeed in dealing with an attack.

There are some good organic fungicides. Try, for instance, 'Safer's Spray'.

Weird bugs and diseases

If you don't recognise a pest, take an affected part of your plant to a retailer for advice. Don't expect too much from them – there are obscure diseases and in some cases even they may not be able to help (see booklist).

Cats

Neighbourhood cats that use your garden as a public lavatory can taint a surprising volume of air and kill those plants that are especially favoured by their attention. They seem to prefer new, expensive specimens.

Prickly things on the soil discourage them – try rose cuttings or holly leaves. Pepper dust works but gets washed away quickly.

If you have a real problem, a non-toxic product, 'Get Off My Garden', sometimes works.

The best solution is an aggressive dog which can get out into the garden when it senses intruders.

Rabbits

They can kill young trees by eating the bark. If they are a problem, buy rabbit-guards (there are many types).

Birds

They will strip berries and the flower buds from fruit trees. There are sprays but black cotton wound around vulnerable plants or netting protect very well without introducing more chemicals into the garden.

Squirrels

Cages might save your fruit crop (but if the animal is city born and bred, it will treat the cage as an exercise frame on which to show off).

149

Dead-heading

If you don't remove flowers which have been fertilised and have become seed heads (dead-heads), the garden may look a bit ragged. But birds love them, and some seeds will sow themselves and come up next year.

However, if you do dead-head some plants which flower throughout the growing season, they will flower more profusely.

Remove the old flower and stalk, leaving the next bud or the first real leaf.

Some roses produce beautifully coloured fruit (hips). Towards the end of the flowering season, it is worth leaving these hips on for added colour in autumn.

Dead-heading rhododendrons and azaleas makes no difference to next year's flowering but it does make the plants look tidier.

Many people remove the old flowers from hydrangeas to tidy up the garden. Don't cut back too far, because the new flower buds are just underneath the old head. If you cut too hard, you'll lose next year's flower.

SUMMARY

These regular jobs are often referred to as maintenance. That's a really depressing idea. Maintenance is not making progress, it's not having fun – it's just keeping the status quo.

If you think of these jobs as optional and as improving your garden, you might enjoy them more and do them more often.

At last, the thrill of weeding, the joy of slug hunting, the ecstacy that is manuring and mulching.

CHAPTER FOURTEEN

Occasional Jobs

Gardening is closely tied into the natural cycle of the year and the calendars, books and articles that detail what to do each month are useful. But they make everything seem so critical: now is the time to prune; this is the last moment in the year for propagation; don't forget to split the herbaceous plants. This turns gardening into a series of duties and obligations.

Gardening needn't be such a heavy burden.

Pruning

Most plants do perfectly without pruning. However, a few trees and shrubs flower or fruit better if pruned – but even these will still grow well enough if you don't do anything to them.

However, each year you don't prune small problems develop. Branches begin to cross and interfere with each other. Air stops circulating inside the plant and diseases and pests take hold. Light doesn't penetrate into the centre, which becomes steadily more unproductive.

The general rule

Pruning is trimming a plant to alter the way it grows so that it produces more flowers, fruit or leaves.

There is an element also of training – cutting the plant so that it grows into a healthy shape. With general pruning this consists of removing spindly growth and encouraging the plant to become bushy from the base.

In most cases it's a fairly delicate and detailed job.

Fruit trees

There are many ways to prune fruit trees. Unfortunately, you can do more harm than good by cutting incorrectly so general guidelines are unreliable. It is safest simply to ask someone who knows or look it up (see booklist). With apples and pears it is vital to know the variety of the tree because although most flower on short spurs of wood at least a year old, some flower on the tips of new growth (among the apples, Discovery, Bramley, Worcester Pearmain).

Once you know what to do, pruning fruit trees is fun and gives good results in terms of increased flowers and better fruit.

Some fruit trees get into a cycle of bearing fruit only every other year ('biennial cropping'). Pruning doesn't cure this: instead, remove two-thirds of the fruit in a fruiting year. Do it early in the season.

Foliage

Only a few foliage plants benefit from pruning. These are mostly the deciduous ones whose spring growth is particularly good.

To encourage this, cut each branch back close to the old stem at the beginning of spring.

Pruning dogwoods in spring also means bright stems in winter.

Examples

cotinus; eucalyptus; dogwoods: willows grown for their leaves.

Plants that flower before mid-summer

These tend to flower on wood grown at least a year before. To make this as strong as possible, remove some of the flowering wood immediately after flowering. The plant will put all its energy into this year's growth – which next year will be ready to bear flowers.

Examples

forsythia; weigela; deutzia; kolkwitzia.

Plants that flower after mid-summer

These usually flower on stems grown in the same year. To get good flowers, encourage the plant to put all its energy into new growth. Prune out older wood at the beginning of the year, cutting back to strong buds.

Examples

lavatera; buddleia; caryopteris.

Hydrangeas

These flower on older wood. If you have a large one and want to reduce its size without losing a year's flowers, prune half the bush one year, half the next.

Wisterias

These flower on short spurs of old wood. So cut most of the stringy growths back to four buds (leave those that are taking the plant in the direction you want it to go). Prune in mid- and late summer.

Rose bushes

These flower best on new growth. In spring, cut the stems down to an outward facing bud. If you want lots of vigorous growth, prune hard (down to five good buds). Since roses hate still, damp air, remove any branch crossing into the centre of the bushes.

Clematis

Early flowering ones (like *C. montana, C. macropetela, C. alpina*)

A light trim is optional after flowering.

Large flowering ones that flower from late May (like 'jackmanii', 'Nelly Moser', 'Ville de Lyons')

In spring, trim each stem back to a swollen bud.

Late flowering species (like *C. orientalis, C. texensis, C. tangutica*)

These flower only on new wood. Cut them down hard in spring leaving about 12 ins above ground.

If the plant is climbing something, simply remove tangled, thin stems in February.

Seeds

The traditional explanation of why people grow plants from seed is that it's cheaper than buying young plants and you can get a greater range of varieties.

But does the money you save on a dozen bedding plants repay the trouble of sowing, pricking out and hardening off?

The real reason most gardeners grow seeds is that it is an enjoyable and organic thing to do. But it's quite a lot of bother and you do need experience to get really satisfactory results.

If you haven't lots of time, there are some seeds that are very easy. These are the 'hardy annuals': clarkia, nemesia, lobelia, alyssum etc.

Sowing hardy annuals
Sow in the garden in spring. Prepare the soil by breaking it up and moistening it. If possible, mix in some multi-purpose compost and make the surface quite fine. Then sow the seed and cover it with its own thickness of soil (small seed needs only the thinnest covering). Put more than one seed in each position – if several come up, you can always take the extra ones out (and maybe put them elsewhere). If possible, protect the seeds from birds with short bamboos with tinsel tied to them.

Sow any left-overs into a seed box or pot so that if there are any failures in the garden you can fill in the gaps.

Don't let them dry out. Since they are delicate and near the surface, water them by sprinkling rather than flooding.

Bulbs

You used to have to lift bulbs after they had died down because a lot of them weren't able to stand our winters. But most newer varieties are now hardy and you don't need to bother.

Some people tidy up their bulbs after flowering by cutting down the leaves. This isn't a good idea because these leaves produce the energy which the bulb needs for flowering the next year. If you remove the leaves too soon, you won't get good flowers the following year.

The best thing to do with bulbs is to feed them. Use high nitrogen feed after they've flowered. That way they will spread and multiply, giving you a clump in the following years.

Propagation

Again, the traditional explanation of why people propagate is that it saves money. The real reason is that it's wonderful to take a piece of plant and get it to root.

If you have never propagated before, try one of the easier plants first. Lavateras, ivies, lavender, thyme and busy Lizzies propagate easily. In summer, cut a length of vigorous new growth about 3in long. Put it in a pot with moist earth and cover with a clear polythene bag to cut down the loss of water. It should root within a couple of weeks: and if it doesn't – you haven't lost anything.

If you are interested in propagation, there are plenty of good books on the subject (see booklist).

Splitting herbaceous plants

There is no harm in letting herbaceous plants grow bigger and bigger. But, at a certain size, the centre of the plant will stop being productive because it is not in contact with fresh earth. If you split it into separate plants, each individual bit will thrive because it has access to soil all around.

This is a excellent way to make a garden look more mature. When you replant the split bits, group them in clumps and plant these around the garden. This makes it look as though the plant is native to the place and springs up naturally here and there.

Of course, splitting herbaceous plants is also a free way of getting more plants.

- You can't split plants which have a single, main root.

- If possible, tease the individual plantlets apart. This works well with many plants including asters, rudbeckias, ajugas, herbaceous geraniums, symphytum and pulmonaria.

- If you can't pull the clump apart, cut it into pieces. Use a knife or a spade, or lever it apart with two forks or trowels (back to back). You'll have to use this technique with plants like hostas, lupins and delphiniums.

- With at least a couple of buds and some root on each lump, the new plant is likely to survive.

Although you can split herbaceous plants at any time they are dormant (from late autumn through to early spring), it is easiest in late autumn when you can see the stems. This also gives the new bits time to recover before they start to grow next spring.

Any bits that don't look big enough to survive on their own can be put in pots. You never know, they might root and then you will have more plants to play with.

The compost heap

Almost every job in the garden produces some organic refuse. If your garden is small, you can probably bag it up and put it out with the domestic rubbish. But this won't work with larger gardens which produce more.

A compost heap is the answer. Not only does it take the waste, it turns it into a great soil conditioner. The process is one of the most magical in the garden.

To be successful with a compost heap, put only organic matter on it (leaves, dead plants or roots). If you treat it as a rubbish dump it will soon become untidy, dirty and nasty.

You can easily build or buy a good compost bin. There are many on the market and making your own is described in most gardening books. It's just a container which is big and tough enough to take rubbish and will withstand the chemicals produced by rotting. To make composting worthwhile, your garden has to produce at least a couple of bags of waste in the autumn.

There is a controversy at the moment within the gardening community about composting. Some advocate good ventilation (lots of holes in the container) while others believe in warm, enclosed composting (no holes in the container). Experiment and join in the fun!

You can speed the process by adding sulphate of ammonia (or a commercial compost activator like 'Garotta'); by mixing the well-rotted compost at the bottom with the fresh stuff every couple of months or by mincing what you put on the heap (see Chapter 15, Tools).

Some things compost badly: unmixed grass cuttings produce sludge; sycamore, lime and plane leaves, woody stems and some thick stalks take a long time. Organic refuse from the kitchen can go on the heap but mix it in otherwise it too becomes sludgy.

Putting the garden to bed

This means preparing the garden in autumn for the winter ahead. This involves pulling up dead annuals, bringing in half-hardy plants (like geraniums and fuchsias), picking up leaves and raking the lawn.

If you don't bother, it doesn't really matter. The garden will be a bit shabby during winter and won't look inviting in the spring. You will probably also have more slugs and disease (they survive the winter in piles of leaves) and will lose tender specimens in the cold.

If you are pressed for time but want to do it, wait until almost all the leaves are off the trees and then do the main clearing jobs in one long session.

Winter

Snow is a good insulator. Don't knock it off plants unless its weight threatens to damage the plant.

SUMMARY

Your gardening year doesn't have to be that busy. There's a few things to do every now and again, but if you miss them, everything will survive.

Many people will find this disconcerting. They are a bit lost without the pressure of obligations, the lists of critical jobs, the panics and hassles.

But free of the pressures, you can do more fun gardening and be more creative. You can improve things rather than just keep them going. You can even go into the garden and simply enjoy it.

158

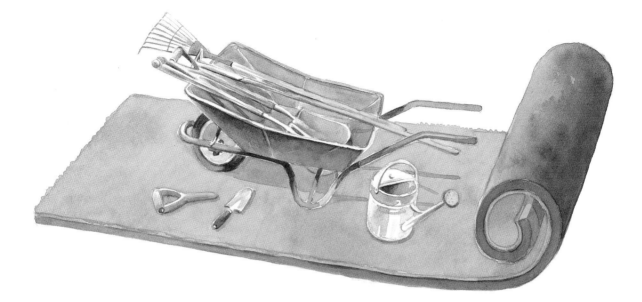

CHAPTER FIFTEEN

Tools

The traditional wisdom is that you should spend as much as possible on tools. But if you do only light gardening, do you really need a costly wheelbarrow? It may be able to shift hundredweights of earth, but you never move that sort of load. It will last many years but, as you don't do heavy work, even your lightweight tools last that long.

The barrow you really need is smaller, lighter and cheaper.

What do you need?

The Instant Gardening rule of thumb is that the more gardening you do, the more you should consider spending.

So if you only garden occasionally and don't get involved with much heavy work, you can make do with less expensive tools that aren't that robust. But these cheaper tools aren't a good purchase if you do more gardening: they can't stand up to heavy loads and regular use. For the committed gardener it usually pays to get expensive tools.

To help people who haven't yet bought a lot of tools, we have divided this Instant tool guide into sections.

Essential tools are those without which gardening is no fun at all. You *can* work without a trowel, but hacking away with a kitchen knife soon becomes depressing.

Useful tools are helpful for those who do lots of work. But you can garden quite satisfactorily without them.

High technology tools are a selection of the modern, often expensive, innovations.

In each case we start with the cheapest and work up to the most expensive.

Because tool suppliers vary so much area by area and year by year, for the most part we give guides to buying rather than names.

Essential tools

Spades and forks

These come in two sizes: standard and border. Border tools are smaller and easier to handle. They are useful for getting into tight spaces.

The cheapest spades and forks are suitable for open soils and for those who don't do too much gardening. These tools feel light when you pick them up. The join between shaft and blade isn't strong and will break if you apply much leverage. Also, the blades of the cheapest spades flex surprisingly easily. They are definitely not suitable for heavier use.

As you rise up the cost range, the tools get heavier. When buying an expensive spade or fork, look for one which is guaranteed.

Wood shafts feel good to work with. They have a nice springiness and are warm to the touch even on a cold day. If the shaft breaks, it can be replaced. Wooden shafts vary in quality and cost: the better ones are made of finer, stronger wood and have a better finish. The best are made of ash.

Metal shafts are often stronger than wooden ones. But if a metal shaft breaks or bends it cannot be replaced and you have to throw away the tool.

The most expensive spades and forks are made of stainless steel. Soil doesn't stick to them, which makes working even clay relatively easy. Also, stainless steel doesn't corrode so they last a long time. If you do heavy work, consider buying one with a wooden (replaceable) shaft.

Trowels

The cheapest trowels are made of pressed metal. They are okay for the lightest gardening, done very occasionally and, at that, only in sandy soil. If you put them under strain too often they will crumple.

More expensive trowels are made of heavier and stronger metal. For most people these are more sensible than the cheapest trowels.

Trowels have a habit of going missing, so the colour of the handle is important. If the handle is green and your beds are densely packed, it's only too easy to lose it. You stand a better chance of finding it if it is, say, white.

The best and, of course, most expensive have stainless steel blades. If you are in the habit of losing tools it may be unwise to splash out on one – although some people find that spending a lot on something means you don't lose it!

Teflon-coated blades are particularly useful in clayey soils as the soil can't stick to them. Another advantage is that they don't corrode.

Secateurs

There are two types: anvil and scissor. The anvil secateur has a single sharp blade which presses against a flat surface; the scissor has two sharp blades which cross.

If you don't do much gardening, buy the best pair of anvil type secateurs rather than a cheap scissor pair because the hinge of the cheapest scissor secateurs is too weak to stand much use.

If you do a fair bit of gardening, or more delicate cutting, the more expensive scissor type secateurs are preferable as they cut more cleanly than anvil ones.

Useful things to look for are:

- wire-cutting notch: if you are likely to cut wire, this prevents the edge of the blade getting chipped.

- swivelling handle: surprisingly effective, especially for heavy work, but expensive.

162

- replaceable parts: you can replace the blades on some secateurs. With others, you have to replace the whole tool. How likely are you to break a blade?

- colour: secateurs are as easy to loose as trowels. Get a pair coloured in such a way that they stand out.

- guarantee: important if the tool is expensive.

- you can also buy left-handed secateurs.

Some secateurs offer the option of a number of settings for different size hands. This is only useful if the secateurs are going to be used by many people. Otherwise the mechanism is a nuisance, as it can easily go wrong.

Try the pair you plan to buy to ensure that they fit your hand.

Hoses

Before you buy hose check your tap so that you can get the appropriate hose-to-tap coupling device. There are many types of taps: mixers, screw thread, universal.

Don't buy too short a length. It makes no sense to have to stretch the thing to reach the far corner of the garden.

There are flat and round hoses. Flat hose is okay if your garden is small and storage space is limited. But it is difficult to use over any length: it kinks easily and you have to unroll the whole length even if you want to water something close to the tap.

For the small garden with limited storage space, you could use round hose stored in a cassette. This doesn't kink as easily as flat hose and you don't need to unroll the whole length to use it. But it's a bit bulkier and comes in limited lengths.

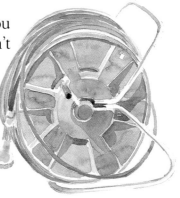

Kinking is a problem even with round hose. The more 'braided' the hose, the less likely it is to kink.

A long guarantee is also a sign that the hose is unlikely to kink – as is higher cost.

You can make your own hose storage system. If, however, you buy a reel and have a fair length of hose, get a heavy duty one as hose can weigh a lot and the reel will break unless well made. This is especially true for wall-mounted reels.

There are many fitments for hoses (see 'Useful tools' following).

Broom

There are two types; stiff and soft.

- Stiff brooms pick up bigger rubbish and move earth off paths. But they don't sweep perfectly clean.

- Soft brooms are like housebrooms. They aren't much use for muddy paths, but can pick up finer stuff.

So if you get the paths dirty and care about neatness, it may be worth investing in both. It will save a lot of hard work.

- Besom brooms (the ones used by witches) look nice and are very cheap. But they always leave bits behind. In unskilled hands this seems to be mostly bits of themselves.

- There are tool systems which consist of a single handle and a number of exchangeable heads. For comments on these 'multiple systems', see later.

Useful tools

Watering fitments
Your hose can be made more versatile by adding a 'universal fitment' to it and various attachments.

Hand held spray attachment
The simplest is an adjustable nozzle which produces a variable spray that can go from a jet to a wide fine mist. These are useful for general watering. More expensive sprayers have an on/off trigger which produces sprays of different densities. These are great for watering things like containers on a patio where you don't want a continous flow. There is an (even more expensive) sprayer with an on/off trigger which produces either a jet or a spray.

Dilutor
Some sprayers have a reservoir for concentrated feed. These are excellent for putting foliar feeds on the garden.

Lawn sprinkler
Invaluable time-saver for watering both lawns and beds. There are many types, the main difference being the area they cover. Check your water pressure before you buy one which makes grand claims: to cover large areas you need good pressure.

Car and patio brushes
Great time-savers. The simplest is a hand-held brush fed by water. They get more complex and expensive, enabling you to wash all sorts of things (greenhouse windows, greenhouse roof, the patio, the poodle . . .)

Wheelbarrows

Barrows are bulky, quite expensive and need somewhere to live. They are only really necessary if you have to move big loads a fair distance.

The cheapest are made of light, pressed metal. They are good for everything but heavier loads.

'Navvy's barrows' are made of much heavier materials and are more costly. They are hardwearing and last a long time. Those with pneumatic wheels are easier to control than those with solid wheels, especially on rougher ground. But you have to be quite strong to enjoy using one.

There are now barrows which are designed like navvy's barrows but with heavy-duty plastic hoppers in place of the metal ones. They are light and strong and fairly easy to control. They are good but rather costly.

The most expensive are 'Ball Barrows'. These have wide spherical wheels which allow you to cross lawns without damaging them. Made of plastic, they don't corrode. You can buy extensions to increase capacity. For all their cost, they are difficult to control when heavily loaded.

Rakes

Rakes with short, rigid claws are useful if you need to make the surface of the earth fine before sowing seeds, level loose soil when laying a lawn, or smooth sand when laying stone.

- If you want to clear leaves off beds, you need a rake with flat, springy prongs.

- To clear leaves off the lawn and pull thatch out of it, the rake needs long wire tines.

- Adjustable rakes are useful because they get into corners and you can pick up finer leaves.

- If you need several rakes, consider the multiple head systems.

Multiple head systems

These are cost-effective if you want to buy several tools which have long handles (rakes, brooms, long-armed pruner etc). They are also sensible if you have limited space for storing tools. Those who can't bend find them convenient too, as every tool is designed to fit on to the end of a long handle.

But they are not that sturdy, so aren't suitable for those who do a lot of heavy gardening.

They make excellent presents, as you can start fairly inexpensively and go on by giving new fitments.

Watering-cans

Watering-cans are no longer one of the essential tools in the garden because most of us have hoses. But if you don't have a hose or need to water pots on a patio and don't want to splash, they come in handy.

The cheapest cans don't give a steady flow of water. This can be really irritating – when they gush, water goes everywhere.

But anything more expensive than the cheapest does the job of delivering water perfectly well.

With the most expensive ones, what you are really paying for is good looks. An enamalled can, for instance, is very attractive and evocative (visions of Beatrice Potter cottage gardens).

This can be a great advantage in a smaller garden where storage space is limited. But in a busy, big garden this is probably not that important as you are likely to have somewhere out of sight to store the can. For these gardens a functional plastic one is usually good enough.

Lawn mowers

You need a mower for anything but the smallest lawn (which can be cut with shears, or even scissors!).

There are lots of mowers on the market. To get the most appropriate, you need to decide how it should cut and what power source you want.

When buying a mower, check where the nearest service centre is, because you don't want to have to cart the machine miles to get it fixed.

How it cuts:

• Cylinder mowers have spinning blades mounted on a rotating cylinder. These make a scissor action against a fixed base plate. They give a fine cut. Cylinder mowers are best for ornamental lawns. They make stripes down a lawn which are made more pronounced when the mower has a roller.

• Rotary mowers have a whirling blade mounted parallel to the lawn. They are more effective than cylinder mowers on coarser lawns and where there are gentle slopes and bumps.

• Hover mowers are specialised rotary mowers, particularly effective on very bumpy or sloping lawns.

Power source:

• Electric mowers are fine for small gardens where the flex is fairly short. But the flex becomes a problem over longer distances.

• Petrol mowers are more bother than electric mowers but better for the big lawn.

• Push mowers give a good cut – but aren't that much cheaper than electric ones.

When buying a mower, check where the nearest service centre is, because you don't want to have to cart the machine miles to get it fixed.

Notes on other useful tools

There are lots of other useful tools. These are the core of a good selection.

Kneelers
Without a kneeler of some sort, weeding and planting out are unnecessarily uncomfortable. You can buy specially made pads which are strapped to each knee. An old cushion seems just as effective.

Lawn spreader
A good way to spread granular preparations on the lawn. If you buy one, remember you'll have to store it between use.

There are now lawn preparations that come in their own dispensers. This seems like a good idea, particularly for the smaller lawn. However, liquid preparations which don't need spreading are much easier to apply.

Bosbag
A large, heavy-duty, non-disposable bag with handles. Marvellous for carrying piles of leaves and bits of plants to the compost heap.

Gloves
As difficult to keep as trowels. Many gardeners dislike wearing them but if you are going to work with anything thorny you'll need a heavy-duty pair.

Shears
Cutting with shears is hard work. The better quality shears are easier to use and cut more cleanly and efficiently. If you have a lot of hedge it is worth investing in an electric hedge trimmer.

Hoes
Good for weeding if you dislike bending.

Sprayers
For a small garden, a hand sprayer is sufficient.

If you've got lots of roses or fruit it is probably worth getting a bigger one which allows you to pump first, then spray continuously.

If you have tall fruit trees or climbers, get one with a long spray nozzle.

Look for sprayers with transparent containers so you can see the level of liquid.

Tool cupboards
If you haven't got anywhere to store tools and don't want a shed, get a tool cupboard. Although small and not walk-in, they keep tools tidy, dry and out of childrens' way.

Saws
Garden saws are used mostly for heavy duty pruning.

A small hand saw is most convenient, preferably one with replaceable blades.

For major branches or felling trees you need a 'bow saw'.

There is a switchblade saw with excellent blades which folds away for easy storage.

Chain saws are great – but dangerous. They are only really necessary if you have a number of trees to tackle.

Long handled pruners
These are useful if you have trees that need pruning. If you also need to pick fruit that grows out of reach, look for a pruner that has a fruit picking attachment.

Some pruners are extendable which makes them much easier to use as you don't have to work with them at their full length all the time.

High tech tools

Hundreds of new gimmicks are launched on to the market every year. Amongst them are a few tools worth considering seriously.

Mincers
These chop organic waste into fine chips. If your garden produces a lot of waste they are excellent, as they reduce the size of compost heap and accelerate the process of composting.

If your garden produces a large amount of waste, buy a powerful (and, yes, that means more expensive) mincer otherwise you'll waste time freeing the mechanism when it jams.

Scarifier
This is an electric rake for pulling thatch out of lawns. Quite astonishingly effective – excellent for big lawns.

You can fit scarifiers to the back of some mowers but they don't do such a good job.

Strimmers
These are used for clearing weeds and edging lawns. The 'blade' is made either of metal or nylon thread.

Those which cut with nylon thread are excellent for the smaller garden and for lawn edging.

Those which have metal blades are more powerful. Use them for clearing hefty weeds (bracken, etc).

Irrigation systems
These are useful for the keen gardener who cannot attend to the garden throughout the year.

The simplest consists of a timer which fits between hose and mains. It turns the water supply on and off.

A more sophisticated system is a computer that fits onto the tap. You can connect all sorts of fitments to it including drip irrigation into pots and hanging baskets, and spray heads with different areas of coverage. Feeds can be added to the irrigation system. Ideal for a small garden.

To fit an irrigation system into a bigger garden, you'll probably have to consider a professional system which incorporates a reservoir and pump. Get expert advice and help if you want one of these.

SUMMARY

Our aim is to help you buy wisely. After all, saving you from making one unnecessarily extravagant purchase could repay, in some cases many times over, the cost of this book!

CHAPTER SIXTEEN

Instant Gardening

Instant Gardening is about how you live and how you might make a garden that suits you. If your children want to practise their jungle fighting skills, the traditional neat lawn and herbaceous beds aren't going to be that important.

Instant Gardening is a completely new way of gardening. If you don't want to grow things from seed – don't. If you have money to spend on high tech tools, using them is not 'cheating' – it's just your way of gardening. If you want a perfect lawn, that's great – and if you don't, that's great too.

Changing your mind and making mistakes are also important parts of Instant Gardening. One of the delights of gardening is that it is one of the few areas of life where you can experiment without doing harm. After all, it is only gardening.

But Instant Gardening isn't a once-off process, done and then put aside. It is something that you can do throughout your life.

Imagine a married couple with a young baby. They move into a house with a sloping, fairly neglected garden. Analysing their resources in the Instant Gardening way they decide to keep the slope, build a sandpit and leave the lawn alone. They rescue some old fruit trees and plant a limited range of clumped specimens which give value all year round.

Within a few years the babies have become energetic young children. Their games wreak havoc with the beds and they tear up the lawn. The sandpit is now redundant. Although the couple want to move house, somehow there's never time and they stay put. Thinking in the Instant Gardening way, they replace the pit with a herbaceous bed, allow the lawn to grow longer and become more robust, and replace the most damaged shrubs with more sturdy specimens.

Then the children become teenagers, mainly interested in sex and themselves. They never go out into the garden. The family still hasn't moved, although there are definite plans to do so in the near future. Until then, however, the parents decide they want a pond. The earth that is dug out of the hole goes into making raised beds which are fronted by makeshift dry stone walls. The wife starts to grow alpines and her husband begins to experiment with grafting on the fruit trees.

174

The years pass and the urgency to move diminishes. So, being Instant Gardeners, the couple employ builders to make a lovely patio and lay some beautiful paths. They decide to reduce the amount of gardening that has to be done, but somehow they still seem to spend more time working outside than relaxing. This isn't so bad – it keeps them fit and healthy.

Then, suddenly, they are grandparents and once again babies toddle around the garden. They contemplate the pond. Is it a danger? How about replacing it with a sandpit?

That's Instant Gardening.

Booklist

Retaining Walls
Jackson and Day, *Outdoors and Gardens*, Collins

Patios
Geoffrey Hamilton, *Garden Stonework*, Foulsham

Michael Lawrence, *Garden Brickwork*, New Holland

Drainage/Lawns
David Pycraft, *The Royal Horticultural Society's Encyclopaedia of Practical Gardening: Lawns, Weeds and Ground Cover*, Mitchell Beazley

Dr D. G. Hessayon, *The Lawn Expert*, PBI

Pollination
Harry Baker, *The Royal Horticultural Society's Encyclopaedia of Practical Gardening: Fruit*, Mitchell Beazley

Training Fruit
Royal Horticultural Society, *The Fruit Garden Displayed*, Cassell

Propagation
Robert Wright & Alan Titchmarsh, *Complete Book of Propagation*, Ward Lock

Philip McMillan, *The Royal Horticultural Society's Encyclopaedia of Practical Gardening: Plant Propagation*, Mitchell Beazley

Wildlife
Chris Baines, *How to Make a Wildlife Garden*, Hamish Hamilton

Pruning
Brian Halliwell, John Turpin & John Wright, *The Complete Book of Pruning*, Ward Lock

Christopher Brickell, *The Royal Horticultural Society's Encyclopaedia of Practical Gardening: Pruning*, Mitchell Beazley

Compost heaps
Sue Stickland, *The Organic Garden*, Hamlyn

General Gardening and Encyclopaedias
Christopher Brickell, *Gardeners' Encyclopaedia of Plants and Flowers*, Dorling Kindersley

John Brookes, *The Small Garden*, C. E. Phillips

Nicola Ferguson, *Right Plant, Right Place*, Pan

Reader's Digest, *Reader's Digest Encyclopaedia of Garden Plants and Flowers*, Hodder & Stoughton

Brian Davis, *Gardener's Illustrated Encyclopaedia of Trees & Shrubs*, Viking

R. Phillips & M. Rix, *Shrubs*, Pan

Index of Plant Names